Dear God

I'm Desperate

Women Have Issues

God Has Answers

Jeanne Le May

ENDORSEMENTS

Finally. A beautifully written resource that honestly and transparently addresses the pressing needs facing women today. No matter their age, race, background, or denomination, readers are wholeheartedly invited to sit in God's lap, pour out their hearts, and receive His words of mercy, truth, healing, and lovingkindness. Thought-provoking questions also allow readers to interact with the text, process their own experiences, and apply God's Word to their lives. This book is a long-awaited answer to every woman's cry for help.

Penny A. Bragg, Author
Co-Founder of Inverse Ministries, Inc.
www.inverseministries.org

Desperate cries that emanate from our souls can leave us breathless and hopeless. Our despair can often pull us into a never-ending quest for answers. *In Dear God I'm Desperate – Women Have Issues, God Has Answers*, Jeanne LeMay beckons us to travel with her on that search.

From personal experience, Jeanne learned that the answers we seek come through the words of God, because He speaks to all real-life issues we all face. Her creative blend of the cries of many women's hearts with powerful scripture thrusts us onto a path of hope—because God hears our cries and knows exactly what to say.

Gail Porter, Author of *Life through Loss*
Co-author of *The Significant Woman*

I LOVE THIS BOOK! Packed full of Biblical wisdom and deep compassion, *Dear God I'm Desperate* addresses a wide variety of issues women face today—stale marriages, adultery, sex addiction, divorce, post-abortion heartache—both inside and outside the church. No topic is off limits.

Author Jeanne LeMay pours wisdom into the content, interlacing the Scriptures throughout God's responses, where He speaks lovingly and perfectly to each woman, tender where needed and firm where appropriate. She provides countless reminders that God understands and cares for us far more than we can imagine. With each heartfelt letter, I could feel the presence of our heavenly Father.

I believe this book will be a gift for many weary, guilt-ridden souls, a huge blessing to many women!

Dena Yohe, Co-founder of Hope for Hurting Parents
Author of *You Are Not Alone: Hope*
for Hurting Parents of Troubled Kids
www.hopeforhurtingparents.com

Jeanne LeMay presents an extensive collection of scenarios faced by today's women. She focuses on God's perspective relative to each difficulty and creatively imparts wise counsel based on God's Word—Truth that never changes no matter the generation or the situation.

Jeanne dug deep into the Scriptures to encourage women to seek God's perfect answer to their cries for help. She draws deeply from within her heart, creating stories that bleed with emotion, leading women to God's fatherly love.

Each scenario reflects a desperate woman's cry for help, and Jeanne leads them to the only One who provides answers to a contemporary woman's issues. She writes with integrity, never saying something God didn't say or promising something He never promised.

Through *Dear God I'm Desperate*, God accomplishes a unique and fresh way to reveal His perfect, never-ending love to his precious, broken-hearted daughters.

Marie Wright, Leader
Inductive Bible Study

In *Dear God I'm Desperate: Women Have Issues, God Has Answers*, Jeanne Le May uses thoughtful insights from God's own Word to answer some of the stickiest issues a woman can encounter. When disappointment and pain wound a woman's heart, Jeanne's beautiful, poignant, and heart-felt words wrap her in a warm embrace of God's love and grace to touch her spirit with comfort and encouragement.

Linda Rooks, Author
Broken Heart on Hold, Surviving Separation
www.brokenheartonhold.com

Dear God I'm Desperate

Scripture quotations are taken from The Life Recovery Bible, an edition of the *Holy Bible*, New Living Translation, copyright © 1996, 2004, 2007, 2013 by Tyndale House Foundation. Used by permission of Tyndale House Publishers, Inc., Carol Stream, Illinois 60188. All rights reserved.

Published by EA Books Publishing a division of
Living Parables of Central Florida, Inc. a 501c3
EABooksPublishing.com

DEDICATION

With special gratitude to:

God my Father.

Dan Penwell for believing in my vision.

Eva Marie Everson for believing in my writing.

Penny Bragg for believing in me.

Marie Wright for setting my spiritual sails in God's direction.

Word Weavers for their expertise and support.

Countless girlfriends who wiped my tears and

All the men that caused them.

ACKNOWLEDGMENTS

*To Mother with love and gratitude
and my daddy who died too young.*

CONTENTS

WELCOME TO HYSTERIA LANE

Welcome to Hysteria Lane, a fictional suburban street where women like us share their daily experiences with family, friends, neighbors, and coworkers.

On the surface, their lives seem amazing, but behind closed doors, circumstances leave their hearts in shambles. Tormenting secrets threaten to shatter their facade of perfection.

Women alone.

Women plagued with depression.

Women distressed with doubts, confusion and fears.

Women struggling with shattered marriages.

Women stunned by bad news.

Women overwhelmed with guilt.

Women heart-broken by children.

Women abused.

God sees. He hears their desperate cries for help as they reveal their deepest sorrows to Him through intimate letters . . .

DIVINE EXCHANGE

At the end of each story, you will have an opportunity to reflect on what you have read, and respond as you apply God's promises to your own life.

You may choose to exchange:

>   Despair for hope
>
>   Worry for peace
>
>   Fear for faith
>
>   Sorrows for joy
>
>   Weariness for strength
>
>   Sickness for healing
>
>   Confusion for clarity
>
>   Anger for forgiveness
>
>   Discouragement for courage
>
>   Insecurity for stability
>
>   Loneliness for comfort
>
>   Rejection for acceptance
>
>   Shame for dignity
>
>   Defeat for victory
>
>   Everything for love

Dear God

Here is where you pour out your heart to our faithful God.

>   What troubles you?
>
>   What is the cry of your heart that you want to tell God?
>
>   What struggle do you face today that needs God's healing, strength and wisdom?

My Dear Daughter

Take a few moments to be quiet and listen to God—the still small voice of His Holy Spirit.

What is God saying to you?

What words from God's truth encourage your weary soul?

What verses from the story deeply touch your heart?

Write down at least one of God's promises from the Bible that assures you of His love and anchors you in His Word.

Example

Dear God,

Today my heart is heavy about my future. I feel so afraid and helpless—I don't know what to do, and I need your help.

My Dear Daughter,

I want you to know that you don't have to live in fear or discouragement over your circumstances. I am with you, and I will help you.

Isaiah 41:10

Don't be afraid, for I am with you. Don't be discouraged, for I am your God.

Jeremiah 29:11

I know the plans I have for you. They are plans for good and not for disaster, to give you hope and a future.

Jeanne LeMay

TEARS ON MY PILLOW

Dear God I'm Desperate

SWEET SIXTEEN AND NEVER BEEN KISSED

Dear God,

Today marks my daughter's sixteenth birthday. Instead of celebrating, my heart trembles, because fifteen years, nine months and seven days ago, I aborted her.

"In no way will you disgrace our family with…with this…baby," Father scorned.

"Young lady, you will not ruin my career with your irresponsible shenanigans. We'll get rid of it before anyone finds out. I'll make the arrangements this afternoon. I'll tell my Board of Directors at the bank that you plan to study abroad this summer. Now, don't you say another word about it."

"Mama, please. Help me."

"Sweetheart, your father is right. Our reputation, you know."

"Mama, I'm so scared. Please don't send me away, Mama. Please?"

"Sweetheart, you'll be fine. The summer will be over before you blink an eye.

Now dry those tears and finish your homework. You'll have to follow your father's decision."

The plot to cover up our shameful family secret began with one discreet phone call. For me, the sabbatical meant three months in the shadows of Father's punishment. Confused and alone, I packed my bags to prepare for an abortion, while my parents planned a party to celebrate my trip "abroad." My junior year ended with spoiled innocence and a farce.

When I arrived at the clinic, a lump formed in my throat. A stranger greeted me with a monologue of questions. As I answered, my voice quivered. With no control, unwelcome tears burst forth, yet there was no one to comfort me. Next, the woman confirmed my appointment with Dr. Johnson for 3:00 p.m. and seated me in the waiting room that seemed devoid of life.

As the nurse explained the prearranged procedure, fear ravaged my heart.

"First, you'll have a physical. Doc J. needs to examine your uterus."

Examine my uterus? My hands trembled.

"We'll order lab tests, including an ultrasound. You'll be sedated so you shouldn't feel any pain. Your cervix may be stretched with dilators."

Stretched. Tube inserted. Suction machine. Suction machine? In less than ten minutes, it will all be done. It? My mind heated with panic as my body froze.

"Your recovery time will take about an hour. You're young. You'll return to normal in no time. Your living arrangements for the next few months are in proper order. Your father already paid and signed the necessary paperwork. Everything is ready now."

As my migraine throbbed, I waited for Dr. Johnson. Alone. Shivering.

The next fall, when I returned to high school as if nothing catastrophic had occurred, I walked through the halls in a hollow trance. As a broken woman among silly girls and immature boys, I didn't belong. Jimmy never knew about the baby—he wouldn't care. My family never mentioned my disgrace again.

During college, I met Steve. As our relationship deepened, I meant to reveal my secret to him, but I feared he would hate me. No occasion seemed appropriate. We are now happily married, but shame still torments my mind. Not a day goes by that I don't imagine my adorable baby.

Would she have Jimmy's smile? My blue eyes? Would her hair be blond like mine or curly like Jimmy's? Would she enjoy ballet? Maybe she's a tomboy.

If only I hadn't…

God, how could I have done such a despicable thing? I'm so sorry. I'll never forgive myself. My heart feels like a rock of black coal. What should I do?

Christina

My Dear Christina,

I have been waiting for you to turn to Me for fifteen years, nine months, seven days, twelve hours, thirty minutes, and three seconds so I could tell you about your precious, beautiful baby you named Amy. Even before I knit her together in your womb,[1] I loved her. As she was placed in My arms, so small and exquisite, I entrusted her to My angels to guard and care for her.[2]

As you cherish thoughts of your daughter, so I cherish thoughts of you, My daughter.

I love you far more than you love Amy. Now that you've trusted Me with your shameful secret and turned away from the scarlet sin[3] of your past, My time to act on your behalf has come. Christina, I forgive you. Totally. Completely. I remove all shame and disgrace. Your heart is now as white as snow.[4]

Take My hand now. I'll hold you close and show you My unfailing love in wonderful ways. Rest as I hold you in My arms and lavish you with My love, for I delight in you.[5] Curl up in My

---

[1] Psalm 139:13
[2] Luke 4:10
[3] Isaiah 1:18
[4] Isaiah 1:18
[5] Psalm 147:11

embrace so I may comfort you and care for you with My tenderness.[6]

Pray to Me, and I promise to listen. As you seek Me with all your heart, you'll find Me.[7] I promise to replace your tears of sorrow with abundant joy.[8] All the distress you're experiencing will be healed, and I will bless your life abundantly.[9]

For I have plans to give you new hope and a future beyond what you can imagine.[10] You will become My hands and My feet, to help other women who struggle with the devastating aftermath of abortion, because you have a special understanding of their needs. Every detail of your nightmare, I will use to reveal Myself to help them.

Your life will become a living sacrifice[11] overflowing with love, a beautiful sight for all to behold. You will flourish like a tree planted along a riverbank, bearing fruit in each season.[12]

Precious Christina, did you realize Amy means Beloved of God?

> Love,
> God

God's Promise: Psalm 30:11

I will turn your mourning into joyful dancing.

---

[6] Psalm 103:13
[7] Jeremiah 29:12-13
[8] Psalm 30:11
[9] Jeremiah 33:6, 9
[10] Jeremiah 29:11
[11] Romans 12:1
[12] Psalm 1:3

Divine Exchange

Dear God

Dear Daughter

NINE ELEVEN

Dear God,

September 11—my daddy's birthday. Why did you let him die when I was only in kindergarten?

Fighting the morning chill, I pulled on my jeans and cashmere turtleneck sweater. The gray-blue color matched my melancholy mood. To counter the onset of depression, I slipped into my pink, fuzzy, oversized slippers. As I scuffed toward the kitchen, I flipped on the TV to see Katie Couric's outfit for today.

Grabbing a steaming mug of decaf, I noticed a news bulletin with the sharp-edged, panic-filled tone of a newscaster's voice, so I tuned a serious ear to the report.

"Burning in the sky, smoke billows from the north tower . . . flames and debris explode from the south tower . . . hijackers crashed two airliners into the World Trade Center in a deadly series of blows that brought down the twin 110-story office buildings . . . many feared trapped . . . rain of debris . . . rubble and ash from the towers cover vehicles . . . towers were leveled . . ."[1]

I could not grasp what I heard. On the large, flat screen, I saw people screaming as they fled for dear life in widespread panic with horror etched on their faces. Sensing tension in my countenance, Muffy meowed as she jumped into my lap.

" . . . residents perched on rooftops, watching smoke rise above the Manhattan skyline."[2]

---

[1] N. R. Kleinfield, *Some Live to Tell Their Stories*, (NY: New York Times, September 12, 2001), Orlando Sentinel, A-6

[2] Dan Tracy, Sentinel Staff Writer, *Attacks Stun Onlookers in New York* (FL: Orlando Sentinel, September 11, 2001), A-6

This was no ordinary birthday for my daddy. By the end of the day, zapped of all strength and understanding, I realized that many children would grow up without their father, too. Like the twin towers, their world was reduced to shambles.

God, what are fathers supposed to be like? Why did you leave me and all those other children fatherless?

Carrie

My Dear Carrie,

I know your heart froze when you saw the devastation of the Twin Towers. No wonder you were horrified by the magnitude of hatred by terrorists that attacked New York with a vengeance. Foundations of many families shattered and broke.[3] Abomination within human hearts brought tragedy to many children that day. I wept.[4]

When you were only 5 years and 54 days old, I saw your sweet face, afraid and confused, when you were told your daddy died. You were left with a heart crushed and dreams buried. I wept that day, too.

[3] Heather Harpham Kopp, *Daddy, Where Were You? Healing for the Father-Deprived Daughter* (MI: Servant Publications, 1998), 66
[4] John 11:35

Don't be afraid, Carrie. I am Father to the fatherless.[5] The instant your daddy took his last breath, I adopted you and chose you to be My own special treasure.[6] I approved and accepted you and embraced you with My love. You are My daughter—signed, sealed and delivered—a special part of My family. I lifted you out of the darkness of that moment into My wonderful light. Now, you belong to Me.

I know you missed the affirmation that a father brings, and you thirst for love. Carrie, please don't be anxious, because I provide all that you need from my unlimited supply. I quench your thirst, because you are valuable to Me. I fill the father-shaped void in your heart.[7] I spend time with you when you cry and when you laugh.

Beyond physical sustenance, I provide emotional nurturing and spiritual stability. I provide protective lines of authority so you are never left wandering in this world without guidance. I nurture you beyond mere existence—I cause you to thrive.[8]

I want you to know this truth, deep down, in your heart of hearts: What happened to your daddy is not your fault. I know your circumstances, and I move among them. I am aware of your pain and monitor your hurting heart every second. I am aware of your emptiness and promise to fill you with My love beyond your wildest dreams. I am aware of your wounds and scars, and I know how to draw forth deep healing. When you feel alone and afraid, I'm here to comfort you.

---

[5] Psalm 68:5
[6] Deuteronomy 7:6
[7] Heather Harpham Kopp, *Daddy, Where Were You? Healing for the Father-Deprived Daughter* (MI: Servant Publications, 1998)
[8] Bryan Davis, *The Image of a Father: Reflections of God for Today's Father* (TN: AMG Publishers, 2004), 20, 36

How precious are My thoughts of you—they cannot be numbered![9] Do you grasp My words? Do you understand how wide, how long, how high, and how deep My love is for you?[10] Allow Me to pour My overwhelming love into your heart to make up for all the years you felt unloved.

Carrie, I am your perfect Father.

Love,
God

God's Promise: Psalm 103:13

The Lord is a father to his children—tender and compassionate to those who love Him.

---

[9] Psalm 139:17
[10] Ephesians 3:18

Divine Exchange

Dear God

_____

_____

_____

_____

_____

Dear Daughter

_____

_____

_____

_____

_____

BLACK TIE AFFAIR

Dear God,

The double mastectomy ten years ago prolonged my life, but now I'm afraid. The recent tests revealed that cancer metastasized beyond surgery. Dr. Horatio says I have two months to live. God, I dread leaving my family behind. My kind hubby. Our two sons, Danny and Joe. And those precious grandchildren. David can't even boil water. He keeps saying, "Honey, everything will be fine. Everything's fine. Don't worry."

But, God, everything isn't fine. I'm not fine. My mind swirls with resentment toward this wretched disease. Pain attacks my body, and I need hospice. Regrets and failures taunt me. Medical bills pile higher each day—cancer has ruined our financial stability. Dreams and plans remain unfulfilled. Watching my innocent grandkids cry breaks my heart. How can I let go?

I hate hospice. I'm not ready to die. God, help me. I'm desperate.

Lisa

My Dear Lisa,

Although you don't know what your future holds,[1] I am Sovereign God[2] who holds your future. As your time on earth draws to a close, your heart lies in the palm of My hand.[3] I promise to sustain you each remaining day of your life.[4] When fears rob

[1] Ecclesiastes 10:14
[2] Acts 4:24
[3] Isaiah 49:15-16
[4] Psalm 55:22

you of peace as you walk through this dark valley, don't be afraid.[5] Seek Me with your whole heart as I prepare you to see Me face to face.[6]

Don't worry about what you leave behind, for My grace is sufficient for your concerns about the past.[7]

David holds no grudge for any slight or angry word. You will now enjoy sweet and tender time together, remembering with laughter and tears your lifetime of shared memories. Then, when your final days draw near, I will gently help him cope with the reality of your passing.

Danny has already forgiven you for rejecting his beloved bride. Although you felt disgraced by her background, her heart remains pure in My sight.

I know you expected Joe to be a doctor like David and your dad, but My perfect plan utilized his artistic gifts. Wait until you see the masterpiece he created for you! And his precious children have been blessed with the legacy of your steadfast faith.[8]

My precious daughter, don't be afraid to let go—I will continue to watch over your family. In your final bittersweet days, continue to proclaim your love for Me. All who gather at your bedside will be captivated by the strength of your faith in your dying hours. My light shining upon your face[9] will remain forever etched in the minds of your loved ones.

When the time arrives for you to join Me, you will have no more pain. No more sorrow. No more tears.[10] The celebration I have prepared for you will be a *black-tie affair* more lavish than a White House banquet. Family and friends in heaven anticipate your arrival. Mama. Daddy. Pop and Gram. Sis is here, too. I know you wondered about her. All those you loved who put their faith in

---

[5] Psalm 23:4
[6] Jude 1:24
[7] 2 Corinthians 12:9
[8] Psalm 112:1-2
[9] Psalm 4:6
[10] Isaiah 25:8a

My Son Jesus Christ long to see your precious face, and so do I.
For I love you with My everlasting love and draw you forth with
My loving kindness.[11]

Love,
God

God's Promise: Psalm 34:4

I pray to the Lord, and He answers me.
He frees me from all my fears.

---

[11] Jeremiah 31:3

Divine Exchange

Dear God

_____

_____

_____

_____

_____

Dear Daughter

_____

_____

_____

_____

_____

CLENCHED JAW

Dear God,

I am 5'2" tall and weigh 171.5 pounds. Every day when Archie comes home from work, he criticizes my body using the exact words hurled at me by my step-dad. My jaw clenches. My muscles clamp into knots. Archie knows I hide in shame because I'm fat, and his mean words cut to the bone. My heart breaks, but I stuff my feelings and eat—more.

Day after day the vicious cycle repeats. With years of unresolved anger, I struggle to feel an ounce of love for Archie. Why can't he simply love me as I am? God, I feel resentful and sorry I ever married *that man*. Will you help me? I'm desperate.

Edith

My Dear Edith,

Because I'm your Daddy, *every* unkind word spoken to you concerns Me.[1] I hear distress in your voice as you cry for help.[2] I can see why you feel resentful, because critical words have pierced your soul. Come now. Hold My hand. Call My name for I am always close. As you share each painful memory, I will comfort you and heal your broken heart.[3] I'll watch over you and help you through this struggle.[4]

Edith, you are wonderfully made. I created every delicate part of you, and My workmanship is marvelous and unique. Like each

---

[1] Galatians 4:6
[2] Psalm 55:17
[3] Psalm 147:3
[4] Psalm 23

17

snowflake, you are one of a kind.[5] I delight in every detail about you—My miracle.

The next time Archie disrespects you with unkind words, say nothing to him. With calm confidence, walk away and meet with Me.[6] Share your suffering. Give Me each tear to cherish. Pour out your hurt feelings, and I will comfort you.[7] I promise to protect[8] you and teach you to respond with My wisdom to those who sin against you.

Now, you need to make a difficult choice. You can continue as a victim and accept his harsh words as true. Or you can cling to My affirmations and promises to you.[9] When you get stronger in My love, I will give you the words you need to speak to Archie with kindness about how his criticism pierces your heart.[10] I will encourage you[11] and never leave your side.

Edith, will you believe Me when I say you are My treasure? I love you exactly as you are now and forever.

Love,
God

God's Promise: 1 Peter 3:9

When people insult you, pay them back with a blessing. Then God will grant you his blessing.

---

[5] Psalm 139:13-14
[6] James 4-8a
[7] Psalm 10:17
[8] Psalm 12:5
[9] Psalm 18:32
[10] Ephesians 4:15
[11] Psalm 138:3

Divine Exchange

Dear God

Dear Daughter

SHUNNED

Dear God,

Mother doesn't love me.

After my divorce, I asked if I could spend Christmas vacation with her. Reluctantly, she said yes. During our visit, our relationship felt strained, but I'm not sure why. Was she ashamed of me for divorce? She's not a woman to discuss her feelings, so I dismissed my concerns realizing the end of my marriage spiked my emotions. I probably overreacted.

The next year went much the same, although my emotions had stabilized.

On the third Christmas visit, tension built to the point of explosion. Her unexplained anger toward me turned to punishing silent treatment. When I tried to share my difficult feelings, she dismissed my efforts and continued to ignore me. After several days of her passive-aggressive behavior toward me, I decided my best choice would be to go home.

Since she was sequestered in her room with the door shut to block communication, I took the next step—called the airline and changed my ticket. We ate separately that day, and I packed my suitcase. We went to bed without speaking.

The next morning, I had hoped to join her for her routine cup of coffee so we could talk, but she had left the house. So I wrote her a note expressing my sadness for how difficult the visit had been for both of us. By noon I still had no word from Mother.

With the flight departing early afternoon, I gathered my belongings, called a cab and waited. Slouching on the porch of the home where I grew up, in my heart I said goodbye to Mother forever. I never felt so lost and alone.

Then Mother pulled her car into the driveway. Time stood still. Two hearts froze.

As she walked toward the porch, she snipped, "I see you're leaving."

"Yes, Mother."

"Well, then, if that's how you see it."

"Yes. It seems best for me to go. I love you, Mother."

The cab arrived. Mother went into the house and slammed the door. I left without looking back. Tears trickled onto my jacket as I wondered if I'd ever see her again.

After the Christmas glitter settled, I tried to call. No answer. No answering machine to leave a message. Week after week I called. No answer. No way to leave a message. She has caller ID, so I knew she was aware of my efforts to reach her.

Finally, in February, she returned my calls. I felt so excited I could have flown, and I answered the phone with a happy greeting.

"Hey, Mom . . .

Immediately she lashed out in a fit of rage, "Why do you keep calling me! I don't want you to call me. Why do you keep calling me! I don't want a call from you. I don't want a visit! I don't want to talk to you. I don't want to see you. Quit calling me."

She slammed down the receiver.

I sobbed like a child.

Lord, I'm desperate. Mother hates me. What should I do?

Brittany

My Dear Brittany,

My daughter, I hear your cries. Come close by Me. I will comfort you with love poured out and doubled. I will never ignore your heartache or shut you out. I'm your safe refuge when you feel rejected. My everlasting arms are under you, holding you.[1] My love covers your sorrow like a shield. As your heart settles, be still and know that I am God.[2] I care for you with gentleness and kindness.

I know you feel neglected and unloved, Brittany, but your mother's choices are not your fault. I know at times she treated you unfairly and favored your sister. Over your lifetime, I've seen her hurl angry words towards you. During the Christmas holidays, I watched as your heart withered with sadness.

I've also seen better times between you—when you laughed and danced. When you blew bubbles celebrating your birthday. When you giggled as you raced around the skating rink. You both also enjoyed a sweet friendship as your mother delighted in your own daughters.

I also witnessed sacrifices she silently made for you over the years and how she struggled without complaint to meet your needs. I saw her cry when you left for college. I comforted her hurt feelings when you shunned her with your teenage attitude. I know your critical thoughts. I held her hand during her lonely times when you have been too busy to notice.

I wept with her through the premature death of your daddy, her beloved husband, when she was very young with three toddlers to support. I witnessed the trauma of widowhood that caused pride-born-of-hurt to harden her broken heart.

My dear Brittany, mothers and daughters often struggle. All little girls frustrate their tired mothers, and well-meaning mothers hurt their daughters. Instead of handling life's ups and downs with compassion and forgiveness, your mother bottled her frustrations.

---

[1] Deuteronomy 33:27
[2] Psalm 46:10

She never experienced My grace.[3] Somewhere along life's difficult journey, your relationship derailed, and strife replaced mercy. But, I know she loves you, because I created mothers with a pure love for each baby gifted them, like the perfect love I have for you.[4] She labored 20 hours before she delighted in seeing your face. She held you first. An indestructible bond was born that day. You are a piece of her heart—breathing, walking, and living.

You have both cried yourselves to sleep many nights because of what happened on that Christmas three years ago. I think it's time for your heart to heal. As you surrender your heartaches and grudges to My loving care, your heart will change toward her, and seeds of reconciliation will be planted.

Brittany, I am your strength and refuge as you take steps to mend the relationship with your mother.[5] You must now influence her for good, rather than let her influence you by holding a grudge.[6] I urge you to forgive your mother.[7] Not to approve of her behavior, but to allow me to judge the entire situation. You must choose to forgive regardless of your feelings, simply because I forgave you.[8] Then you will both be blessed.

In My sight, you are both precious jewels.

Love,
God

God's Promise: Exodus 20:12

Honor your father and mother. Then you will live a long, full life in the land the Lord your God is giving you.

---

[3] Acts 15:11
[4] Jeremiah 31:3
[5] Jeremiah 16:19
[6] Jeremiah 15:19
[7] Exodus 20:12
[8] Colossians 3:13

Divine Exchange

Dear God

_____

_____

_____

_____

_____

Dear Daughter

_____

_____

_____

_____

_____

WITHERED HEART

Dear God,

Jake, my best friend and true love and husband—gone forever. Even after all these months, my heart aches. Never-ending pain pounds my head by day, and rivers of tears drench my pillow by night.

What's the point of going on? At work, simple tasks zap every ounce of my energy. With no interest in friends or hobbies, I sit for hours in a stupor. When I try to eat, I can't stand as much as the thought. My clothes sag like my eyelids. Sunsets and songs no longer matter. A gray mist of numbness encompasses me no matter where I turn. When Jake died, my heart withered.

God, I feel so alone. Will there be no end to my sorrow?

Danielle

My Dear Danielle,

My precious child, I see your tears and know the endless depth of your pain. Jake's death splintered your heart, left you feeling vulnerable and changed the entire landscape of your life. Nothing remains the same.[1] I hear you cry as you struggle through each lonely day and dark night.[2]

Facing endless tangled emotions alone seems impossible to bear. Lack of concentration plagues you. Anger and resentment cause you to blame everyone in your path for what they did or did

[1] Penny A. Bragg, *For Those Who Weep—A Grief Response Journal,* www.forthosewhoweep.com
[2] Psalm 46:1

not do for Jake. Hurtful words spoken and actions not taken grate your nerves.

Danielle, as you ponder the magnitude of your loss, difficult emotions are natural. When those unwanted feelings creep in, reach for Me to bless you with comfort.[3] With each heartache, come to Me, and I will blanket you with hope.[4]

I will never criticize you in your grief as you have experienced from impatient family and friends. Instead, I gently protect[5] your heart. I listen without condemnation[6] and guide you[7] through your darkest moments. No matter what other people say or think, there is no shame[8] in your feelings of desolation. Needing help during this season of mourning indicates no weakness on your part.[9]

Marriage to Jake has been the center of your life for the past fifteen years. And now, for reasons you may never understand,[10] he rests peacefully forever in My care.[11] You resist joy, but in due time, you will come to understand that moving forward in your life neither betrays Jake nor erases him from your memory.

In the meantime, Danielle, you are not alone.[12] As the weariness of grief heaps its heavy toll, I remain your refuge and strength.[13] My daughter, with painstaking care, I will gently create a different design from the shreds of your former life as I comfort and heal your broken and discouraged heart.[14] My warm, intimate embrace always awaits to envelope you.

---

[3] Matthew 5:4
[4] Hebrews 6:19
[5] Matthew 11:29
[6] Romans 8:1
[7] Psalm 32:8
[8] Isaiah 54:4-5
[9] Ecclesiastes 3:1, 4
[10] Isaiah 55:8
[11] John 3:16
[12] Jeremiah 49:11
[13] Psalm 46:1
[14] Rebecca Carpenter, *Ambushed by Glory in My Grief*, Central FL: EA Books Publishing, 2016, 84

Come to Me now, My beloved, and allow the endless depth of My love[15] to seep into the sad-shaped hole in your heart.

Love,
God

God's Promise: Revelation 21:4

He will wipe every tear from their eyes, and there will be no more death or sorrow or crying or pain. All these things are gone forever.

---

[15] Ephesians 3:18-19

Divine Exchange

Dear God

_____

_____

_____

_____

_____

Dear Daughter

_____

_____

_____

_____

_____

MADISON

Dear God,

It's been a tedious year fraught with anxiety. Pain still grips my heart as I remember the horrible moment Dr. Beckwith delivered the fatal news. With trembling hands, I lifted Madison's still, fragile body from her basinet. Tiny fists, with fingernails almost too small to see, were clinched. High upon her left cheekbone, a faint brown birthmark captured my heart. She was perfect.

God, why did you steal her from me? I'm supposed to be a mother, but no child calls for me in the night.

At the funeral, she wore a delicate, silk Christening gown with hand embroidery and exquisite pearls. The matching bonnet covered a wisp of blonde hair. Long lashes lined her closed eyelids. She rested as if frozen in the tiny coffin, oversized compared to her premature body. I studied her pale, porcelain face.

Today, Madison's first birthday, the silence of her empty nursery lures me inside. The pink ruffled sheets still adorn the crib as if she'll be home tomorrow. All the necessities—diapers, baby powder, and booties—remain untouched. Stuffed animals wait in every corner. As I open the closet filled with pink dresses, my stomach churns. I sit alone on the rocking chair covered with the velvety-soft blanket that never held her.

God, I'd rather die than face another day without Madison. My empty heart never stops longing for my precious baby. Without her, life seems hopeless.

Nicole

My Dear Nicole,

During this darkest season of your life, I felt your grief as I watched over you.[1]

Although you felt anger toward Me, I never moved from your side.[2] Nor did My eyes stray from your sorrow. I tasted the salt of your tears, and I held the lifelessness of your heart close to Mine.[3]

I know how excruciating this loss has been for you. I see you cry yourself to sleep each night missing your precious Madison. Come to Me now. Let Me gently rock you and bring you comfort.[4] Close your eyes. Listen and rest in this vision I share with you.

Nicole, picture that you're floating across the heavens as if running in slow motion. Bundled in a soft blanket, Madison peacefully sleeps in your arms—tiny and perfect. Over the clouds, you drift toward Me with the gentle breeze.

As you approach My throne of grace[5] framed by the glow of an emerald rainbow,[6] I greet you with kindness and open arms. Awe of My magnificence overwhelms you with joy, and a single tear slides down your face. As you bask in My overpowering love for you, without hesitation or reservation, you hand precious Madison to Me for My constant care and protection. With a smile, I enfold her in My gentle embrace.

Nicole, when you awaken, your dim room will remain quiet. Peace which surpasses human understanding will flood your heart and soul.[7] You will know without a doubt that sweet Madison rests in My everlasting love. All along she has been safe in My arms. But how could you possibly see, blinded by tears?

Now that you have released your beloved baby to Me, the time has come for your heart to also find peace in My love. Rest assured

---

[1] Psalm 33:13-14
[2] John 14:16
[3] Isaiah 40:11
[4] Psalm 10:17
[5] Hebrews 4:16
[6] Revelations 4:3
[7] Philippians 4:7

that she remains with Me always. She's waiting for you, smiling with dimples like yours.

Nicole, whenever you are ready, you, too, may smile once again, for I love you both beyond measure.

Love,
God

God's Promise: Psalm 56:8

> You keep track of all of my sorrows. You have collected all of my tears in your bottle. You have recorded each one in your book.

Divine Exchange

Dear God

_____

_____

_____

_____

_____

Dear Daughter

_____

_____

_____

_____

_____

HEADACHES ON HYSTERIA LANE

Dear God I'm Desperate

HOW TO SHOP FOR A MAN

Dear God,

On Hysteria Lane, I'm the only woman who has never been married. Some call me an *old maid*, but I prefer the label of *single*. At 37 years young, I can't believe I still haven't met Mr. Right.

Every relationship begins with excitement and promise but soon ends in disappointment and heartbreak. Although I get discouraged, I still have hope for finding a man to love me for the rest of my life. God, how on earth do I shop for a man?

Ashley

My Dear Ashley,

I understand your desire for a husband to share your life happily-ever-after. I also delight in granting desires of your heart when they are best for your well-being.[1] I know your quest for a suitable husband seems daunting—like shopping for a diamond.

How do you distinguish real from artificial?

Is the gem that catches your eye worth the price?

How can you detect flaws and find high quality?

---

[1] Psalm 21:2

Since I created both diamonds and men, I would love to help you. Experts rate diamonds based on *color, clarity, carat* and *cut.* This criteria could also be applied to evaluating a man's suitability as your husband. So together let's explore the possibilities.

The *color* of a rare diamond is in fact colorless, and light shines through easily. Because variations seem subtle and difficult to detect, a trained eye must determine true transparency. Likewise, to find a Godly man of excellent character, you will need divine intervention.[2] With My wisdom, you may discern a man's honesty, integrity and true transparency in order to see My light in him.

Clarity of a diamond reveals both surface and internal imperfections. Defects range from slightly visible to blatantly obnoxious, and flaws disrupt the flow of light and decrease value. Gemstones with surface blemishes and inclusions are common, unsightly, and undesirable. Likewise, men with poor conduct such as drunkenness, immorality, and outbursts of anger must be avoided.[3] On the other hand, a valuable diamond with a polished surface contains minimal inclusions, and a man of good character exudes kindness, gentleness and self-control inside and out.[4]

Carat of a diamond, often mistaken for size, also determines worth. Two diamonds of equal carat-weight could differ greatly in value if one has additional, desirable attributes. So it is with men, Ashley, so be careful. First impressions can be deceptive, and a shallow choice reaps difficult consequences. On the other hand, ethical principles always create added value. Would you trade faithfulness, patience and peace for wealth, power, and appearance?

---

[2] 2 Peter 1:3
[3] Galatians 5:19-21
[4] Galatians 5:22

Cut is the most important criteria to consider in selecting a high quality diamond. A stone with poor workmanship that deviates from the ideal standard, reveals a dark center, appears lifeless, and reflects no light. Likewise, choosing a man based on fluctuating cultural preferences and lack of commitment always results in disappointment. Conversely, a well-cut diamond reflects light. A husband *cut* from My cornerstone chiseled in My image reflects My light and exudes a brilliant radiance.

Ashley, choosing a diamond or a life partner involves careful evaluation, so I advise you to painstakingly consider every detail of a man's character. With variables extensive and trade-offs risky, making a choice on appearances alone may lead to deception and give a false impression of a great deal.

Value of a man's character depends on the interplay of many traits, so compare for quality under the magnification of My Word. A man of Godly character will always delight in encouraging you and protecting you as he depends on Me as his true source of life.

In the meantime, My precious daughter, how have you prepared to become a wife of noble character?[5]

Let's examine your *color*. Does My light shine through you?

Let's examine your *clarity*. Have you allowed me to remove your internal flaws? Have you renewed your mind with My precepts and love?

Let's examine your *carat*. What *added value* do you offer a Godly man?

Let's examine your *cut*. Do you deviate from My standards and reveal a dark center, or are you chiseled in My image reflecting My light with brilliant radiance?

---

[5] Proverbs 31

Ashley, I created you as a brilliant solitaire—one of a kind jewel of exquisite quality—whether you marry or remain single. If you commit your love to another, set your standards high. Rely on Me to direct your path, and I will lead you to best serve Me utilizing your spiritual gifts.

You are worthy of genuine love.[6] Search for Me with all your heart, for I AM the Bridegroom of your dreams [7].

Love,
God

God's Promise: Matthew 6:33

Seek the Kingdom of God above all else, and live righteously, and He will give you everything you need.

---

[6] Jeremiah 31:3
[7] Exodus 3:14

Divine Exchange

Dear God

Dear Daughter

IN MONEY WE TRUST

Dear God,

Tom and I jointly earn $75,250 per year—that sum should meet all of our needs. But in reality, we spend more than our monthly combined paychecks. First, Uncle Sam deducts a huge chunk. Then the mortgage debits electronically. When we total our credit card minimum payments, including the outrageous interest, they devour a disproportionate amount of money.

We are left with only $500 cash each month to divide between groceries, clothing, health care, soccer, iPhones, gas, and everything else necessary to maintain our good life on Hysteria Lane. Instead of planning a bright future for our family, we dug a financial grave.

Recently I noticed "In God We Trust" on a dollar bill. When I told Tom, he said, "That must be a sign. Why don't we ask Him?"

God, can we trust You concerning our money?

Cindy

My Dear Cindy,

Yes. You and Tom can trust me with your money.

My question to you is, "Can I trust you with My money?"

You see, Cindy, your belief system is based on the *lie* that you own everything you possess. The truth is, everything created belongs to Me.[1] Your house is Mine. Your technology, cars, and

---

[1] Psalm 89:11

every dollar you earn—all these things I have entrusted to you for My purposes.

The hardest part of facing your monumental debt is to admit the truth—by mismanaging money, you became a servant to your lenders.[2] Your spending is out of control. You fell into the common temptation to be rich and got trapped by many foolish and harmful desires that plunged you into ruin and destruction. Your love of money is the root of all kinds of evil. Craving what money can buy, you wandered from your true faith and pierced yourselves with many sorrows.[3]

Yet, have you and Tom agreed on a solution? No. You became trapped in a web of trouble.[4] Creditors in constant pursuit of late payments sling threats at you like hot coals heaped upon your head. Debt swallowed your dignity.

Cindy, there is no easy way to say this—you and Tom have fallen short of My standards regarding your finances for years. In spite of your failures, I am a God of compassion and mercy, slow to get angry and filled with unfailing love and faithfulness toward you.[5]

Now that you both have repented, I forgive you.[6] Although you failed to manage My resources wisely, I delight in blessing you with a new start and restoring your joy.[7] The time has come for you to take a leap of faith to obey my commands regarding money.

First, always bring your tithe to Me—$7,525 this year. I know that seems like a staggering amount based on what you gave last year. But, if you do, I will open the windows of heaven for you. I will pour out a blessing so great you won't have enough room to take it in.[8]

---

[2] Proverbs 22:7
[3] 1 Timothy 6:9-10
[4] Job 36:8
[5] Psalm 86:15
[6] 1 John 1:9
[7] Romans 4:7
[8] Malachi 3:10

Second, depend on Me instead of money for your security. For no one can serve two masters. Either you will hate the one and love the other, or you will be devoted to the one and despise the other. You cannot serve both Me and money.[9]

Third, keep your lives free from the love of money, and be content with what you have.[10] Instead of feeding your greed, bless others. Share your food with the hungry. Give clothes to those in need. Provide shelter for the homeless.[11]

My precious daughter, try My ways. Put Me to the test.[12] When you do, you will find both financial freedom and peace of mind.

Love,
God

God's Promise: Proverbs 11:28

Trust in your money and down you go! But the godly flourish like leaves in spring.

---

[9] Luke 16:13
[10] Hebrews 13:5
[11] Isaiah 58:7
[12] Malachi 3:10

Divine Exchange

Dear God

Dear Daughter

SISTER ACT

Dear God,

Ever since we were kids, Heather earned my admiration. She's smart, funny and caring. When I started kindergarten, she held my hand in silence on the ugly yellow bus. Then she helped me find my classroom.

During grade school years, we hid under the covers and whispered secrets. We danced through the house wearing pink tutus and ballet slippers. She taught me to draw and paint.

Every birthday as far back as I can remember, we blew out our birthday candles together.

As budding teenagers, we squealed with excitement at our first rock concert and giggled at jokes that only the two of us understood. When our parents divorced, we cried alone together. No matter what I needed, Heather eased my fears.

The moment she left home to attend University, I felt a huge sense of loss. For the first time in my life, I traveled to the beat of my own drum—not one orchestrated by Heather. Ever since that day, we have marched out of sync. Heather lost interest in my life.

Out of necessity, I discovered my own identity, separate and distinct from Heather. I joined the Wildcat Marching Band and made new friends. Week after week, she paid no attention until months high-stepped into years. She still has no interest in my life. My broken heart has a Heather-sized hole.

Our lives, once intertwined with affection and delight, seem divided by a chasm of hurt and pain. I take interest in her life, but she never reciprocates. She hurts my feelings over and over like a bad habit. God, I'm desperate. How do to get Heather to love me again? I'll do anything—I just want my sister back.

Kayla

My Dear Kayla:

I understand how sad you feel without Heather in your life. Missing shared intimacies, you feel lost. Losing a relationship with your sister hurts. Grieving seems harder when the one you love is physically present but has *chosen* to reject you by withholding her heart.[1]

You shared life-experiences with Heather unlike any other person. With priceless memories, you are left grieving with no hope for your future to include her.[2] Kayla, I know you feel unimportant, sad and helpless.

Because your heart is tender, My advice for you will seem difficult—you must wrestle with how to forgive Heather for hurting you.[3] When you are ready to make that choice out of obedience to Me, you will be set free in spirit.[4]

Kayla, as you forgive and hope for reconciliation,[5] may I introduce you to another dear sister? Not to replace Heather, for who could do that? Her name is Wisdom.[6] With a pure heart and peace-loving spirit, she will lead you along straight paths[7] as you grieve and heal.

Wisdom, full of mercy, considers your needs.[8] Her vitality for life bubbles forth like a brook.[9] She brings light to your eyes and

---

[1] Psalm 145:9
[2] Genesis 16:13
[3] Matthew 6:14
[4] John 8:32
[5] Psalm 133:1-3
[6] Proverbs 7:4
[7] Proverbs 4:11

softens your face.[10] Nothing you desire can compare with her for she is more precious than rubies,[11] better than jewels of pure gold.[12] Wisdom protects, and preserves your life.[13] She's priceless—better than a substantial inheritance.

Wisdom, sweet to your soul, offers hope for your future.[14] She promises to watch over you as Heather did when you were children.[15] Kayla, will you love her as your sister?

Love,
God

God's Promise: Proverbs 17:9

Love prospers when a fault is forgiven, but dwelling on it separates close friends.

---

[8] James 3:17
[9] Proverbs 18:4
[10] Ecclesiastes 8:1
[11] Proverbs 8:11
[12] Proverbs 16:16
[13] Ecclesiastes 7:12
[14] Proverbs 24:14
[15] Proverbs 4:6

Divine Exchange

Dear God

_____

_____

_____

_____

_____

Dear Daughter

_____

_____

_____

_____

_____

VICIOUS CIRCLE

Dear God,

I hate arguments. With any confrontation, tension penetrates every fiber of my body like an electric shock. Unsolicited anger grates my nerves, and I react defensively. Exasperated, I explode with harsh words. Then I suffer from guilt, knowing I was wrong. Shame shrouds me like a blanket of smog. Angst strangles my heart.

God, I'm desperate. How can I break this vicious cycle of anger?

Abi

My Dear Abi,

You have made a wise choice to surrender your anger to Me, for I have given you every emotion for a reason. Let's take a moment to examine the cause of your aggravation. Then I'll teach you how to choose wise responses instead of angry reactions in confrontational situations.

For example, frustration gives you an indication that something may be wrong. Guilt leads you to ask for forgiveness when you have hurt other people. Righteous indignation serves as a barometer to determine the presence of sin—anger could indicate an injustice.

One day My son entered into the house of worship and found merchants and money changers crowding out the people who had come from all over the civilized world to worship. They cheated foreigners who didn't know the exchange rates and thwarted people's attempts at worship.[1] Their deceitful commercialism stripped the temple of all dignity and respect. Confrontation became necessary to break the destructive cycle of behavior.

Sometimes unconditional love requires discipline and accountability, rather than permissiveness, passivity and weakness. In your relationships, a line of respect must be established. What is and is not acceptable behavior? When instances of disrespect are permitted to pass unnoticed, the offender may be unaware that he has stepped over the line and repeats the indiscretion later,[2] like a dog returns to its vomit.[3]

After the conflict in the temple, My constructive teaching followed. I said, "My temple is a house of prayer for all nations, but you have made it a den of robbers."[4] With an attitude of love, I clarified limits to reestablish respect for Me and My house of prayer.

When you feel your anger rise within, call My name. Reflect on what I have taught you. Instead of exploding, follow My example, and I will refine your temperament and inappropriate behavior.

With the gentleness of a dove,[5] point out the sin to the one who has hurt you. Be careful not to insult him in your confrontation. Instead, direct your objection against the wrong behavior. Maintain quiet dignity, self-confidence, and common courtesy in your demeanor. Most important, don't sin by letting your anger control you,[6] for a fool gives vent to his anger, but a wise man keeps himself under control.[7]

---

[1] Mark 11:15-16

[2] Dr. James C. Dobson, *Love Must be Tough: New Hope for Families in Crisis* (TN: W Publishing Group, Division of Thomas Nelson, Inc., 1996)

[3] 2 Peter 2:22

[4] Mark 11:16-17

[5] Matthew 10:16

My precious daughter, never allow others to shame you when they sin against you. Do you not know that My Spirit lives within you?[8] I come to your defense when you are defiled, because you are wonderfully made and precious in My sight.[9]

Love,
God

P.S. Abi, your name that I chose especially for you means *Father's Joy!*

God's Promise: Isaiah 41:10

> Don't be afraid, for I am with you. Don't be discouraged, for I am your God. I will strengthen you and help you. I will hold you up with my victorious right hand.

---

[6] Psalm 4:4a
[7] Proverbs 29:11
[8] 1 Corinthians 6:19
[9] Psalm 139:14

Divine Exchange

Dear God

Dear Daughter

WORN SOULS

Dear God,

The problem with Sarah plagues me. She begged to bring her children to live with my family. I know she's my sister, but the nerve of her thinking she could bring her ragamuffin, runny nose kids to our home—*from living on the streets.* What kind of germs and diseases would they carry? What would the neighbors think? This gated community keeps riffraff *out* of our midst.

Our large home could accommodate extra people, but Sarah caused her own problems. I warned her not to marry Loser Larry—he would cause nothing but problems. Now she expects me to bail her out.

God, Sarah's problems aren't mine. How do I say no?

Taylor

My Dear Taylor,

I'm delighted to hear from you. You're more special to Me than the exquisite pearls you bought in Tokyo last summer. The qualities I love about you are more numerous than the dozens of shoes in your closet. Your value to Me exceeds that of all the antiques in your collection. How I've missed you!

All your life, Taylor, you have been showered with bountiful material blessings. Come. Let's walk and talk. It's been too long. I'd like to read you a special letter I received last week—from your sister. Listen carefully as I share. Then you will know what to do. Sarah writes,

> *Dear God,*
>
> *My name is Sarah.[1] I know you don't remember me, but, with Christmas around the corner, I thought of You. Stores shine with festive decorations. Santa promises children he will deliver their heart's desire. How I hate this season of the year. I can't even feed my children— toys are out of the question.*
>
> *My heart aches as I watch my barefoot children. They have outgrown their only pair of shoes. The soles of mine have thinned from walking three miles to the library to read. Sometimes we stop by a local church to beg for food and rest. I often carry Scotty and Alicia, because their little legs wear out. We camp in the woods to hide from scowls and questions that hurt us. But now, with cold weather, I worry about keeping my precious babies warm. We have no coats. No blankets.*
>
> *Memories of last year haunt me as I picture them running around the trailer searching for presents. Ali and Scotty still believed in Santa Claus and expected presents, because he didn't need money. But they found nothing. When they approached me with downcast eyes, my heart ached.*
>
> *"Mom, we must have been bad. Santa forgot us."*
>
> *God, my heart broke. Society etched a cruel mark on their hearts. They believed they were bad, because I couldn't afford to give them presents. I felt like a failure. Later that night Larry beat me again, so the next day I packed a few things in a paper bag, gathered the children, and left.*

---

[1] Sarah F. Harris, *Cast Aside*, Light & Life Magazine (IN: Free Methodist Church of North America, March-April, 2007), Pull-Out.

Now, with no husband, I alone bear the sadness in the eyes of my babies. With no income, we walk the streets. I search for items discarded by the affluent to survive. One lucky day, I found a few toys—now adopted and loved by my children. A truck for Scotty. A worn teddy bear for Ali. And a mat to lie on rather than sleep on the ground.

Before finding the campground, we moved from a trailer to a run-down shack. Then we lived three months in the battered, abandoned Ford Escort. When the weather got unbearably hot, the kids and I spent time wandering through Walmart for air conditioning. If I watched carefully, we could sneak a bath without getting thrown back into the streets.

God, most people pretend that nobody goes without a meal. To them, we're invisible. Nothing hurts me more than the looks of disdain given by upstanding individuals who surround us. I feel like community-refuse tossed aside through no fault of my own. With local shelters full and abuse centers turning me away, how do I care for my children?

Out of desperation, last week I swallowed my pride and called my sister from the library phone.

"Taylor, would you spare us a small room so I could clean up and find a job. Then we'll move on. I just need a chance to get on my feet again."

"Wow, Sarah, I'm sorry you're having trouble, but we have a lot of important entertaining planned for the holidays. Clients. You know. Anyway, why don't you call again in January. Maybe we can help then. Sorry, Sarah. Bye. Gotta go."

The dial tone blared in my ear. Right. January. I'll call on my new cell phone—if we aren't dead by then. As I hung up the receiver, I said to absolutely no one, I will provide for my children. Somehow. There must be a way.

God, do you care? I can't hear you over our growling stomachs. I can't feel you when we shiver with cold. I can't see you because suffering fills my eyes.

I have nothing to offer—except myself. I'll find a willing man and trade for tonight's room and board. . . Later that night, for the first time in years, my head rested on a pillow. Tears of shame silently stained the covers, as I wondered, Oh God, what have I done? Will you help me? I'm desperate.

Sarah

Taylor, the letter you just read expresses the cry of your sister's heart. Now I say to you, whatever you choose to do for Sarah, you do for Me.[2]

Love,
God

God's Promise: Psalm 41:1

Oh, the joys of those who are kind to the poor! The Lord rescues them when they are in trouble.

---

[2] Matthew 25:34-46

Divine Exchange

Dear God

_____

_____

_____

_____

_____

Dear Daughter

_____

_____

_____

_____

_____

SHALLOWEEN

Dear God,

The Halloween holiday seems out of hand. In September, before I get the kids off to school, Halloween paraphernalia drapes the store shelves. Fancy chocolate witches and ghosts haunt and tempt us. Strings of lights, shaped like dead-man's bones, clothe the store aisles. Dreadful costumes lurk in every store window.

By October, Hysteria Lane resembles a graveyard. Lawns decorated with devils and demons prepare to scare trick-or-treaters. After dark on Halloween night, haunting noises creak from foreboding doorways. Children beg for candy from anybody despite the fact that we teach them not to speak to strangers.

The Bible warns us to avoid all sorts of occult—witchcraft, sorcery, psychics, divination, and consulting mediums.[1] Yet everyone celebrates these activities during October, and fear masks as fun. God, I feel confused. What am I to believe about Halloween? How do I celebrate?

Morticia

---

[1] 2 Chronicles 33:6

My Dear Morticia,

I can see how events surrounding SHalloween confuse you. Because of your spiritual maturity, you desire to evaluate the phenomenon from the backdrop of your faith. You are right—evil lurks masked as fun. When you discern truth, you know whether a celebration is good or bad for you.[2]

The origin of Halloween goes back 2,000 years before the days of Christianity to a practice of ancient Druids. The Winter Festival honored their god, Samhain, Lord of the Dead.[3] As part of the celebration, people donned grotesque masks and danced around bonfires pretending they were pursued by evil spirits. If the evil spirits did not get a treat, they would trick the living.[4] Human sacrifices were offered, and people engaged in occult arts. Long ago the people who worshiped statues and nature also believed that the spirits of the dead could control the living.[5]

Halloween today is a very serious observance for true witches, neo-pagans and other occultists. Halloween also prompts children to pull out a Ouija board and attempt to contact spirits of the dead, which is anything but an innocent pastime, to get people to look somewhere besides Jesus Christ for answers.[6]

So you can see, Morticia, in some instances, the observance of SHalloween is not an innocent practice and represents more than a day of children's tricks or treating. The truth is, there is a spiritual battle between the kingdom of God and the kingdom of Satan. Therefore, dabbling in the occult is anything but a harmless

[2] Linda Hacon Winwood, *Mommy, Why Don't We Celebrate Halloween?* (PA: Destiny Image Publishers, Inc. 2003), 2

[3] Josh McDowell and Don Stewart, *The Occult: The Authority of the Believer Over the Powers of Darkness* (CA: Here's Life Publishers, Inc., 1992), 200

[4] Ibid, 199

[5] Linda Winwood, *Mommy, Why Don't We Celebrate Halloween?* (Destiny Image, 2015), 7

[6] Josh McDowell and Don Stewart, *The Occult: The Authority of the Believer Over the Powers of Darkness,* (CA: Here's Life Publishers, Inc., 1992), 6, 7, 13, 14

Jeanne LeMay

pastime, and to associate your child with such practices, even indirectly in humor or jest, is unwise.[7]

Fortunately, SHalloween, as most commonly practiced today, no longer supports occult activities. I will not condemn you for participating in a purely secular pastime that can be engaged in without any occult associations at all.[8]

I know that you do not *support the occult* by dressing Ben as a bunny rabbit for trick or treating. However, you must strongly question the advisability of allowing Ben to dress up as genuine occult character—witch, wizard, or devil—or to dress in any manner that could bring dishonor to Me. With that in mind, I ask you, Morticia, *what* are you celebrating? *Why* are you celebrating? What alternatives could you consider?

To avoid confusion, you need My wisdom and discernment to avoid choices that seem innocent but could become spiritually compromising. As you weigh the evidence, rely on My Spirit to guide you.[9] Following Me may mean that you leave some traditions behind. What the culture regards as important often differs from My priorities, and what may be a matter of conscience for you may not be the same for others.[10]

Identify your motives. Examine your heart, and test everything against My word. Hold on to the good as you avoid every kind of evil[11] detestable in My eyes.[12] Be sure your choices don't cause anyone of lesser faith to stumble.[13]

---

[7] John Ankerberg & John Weldon, *The Facts on Halloween*, (OR: Harvest House Publishers 1996), 16
[8] Ibid,18
[9] 1 Corinthians 1:18-29
[10] 1 Corinthians 10:29
[11] 1Thessalonians 5:21-22
[12] 2 Chronicles 33:6
[13] 1 Corinthians 10:32

59

Be aware of Ben's feelings, too. If he seems frightened, take his fears seriously. Reassure him that you will do all you can to protect him from harm. [14] As you trust in Me, you will know what is right for you, for everything is permissible, but not everything is beneficial.[15]

This SHalloween, I invite you knock on My door and spend time with Me. You don't need a costume at My house—just come as you are. Instead of wearing a mask, let your face radiate with My light. When you choose to bring honor to Me,[16] you will be treated to many blessings better than a sack filled to the brim with candy.

I love you. No tricks. For I am God, and there is no other.[17]

Love,
God

God's Promise: Matthew 7:7

Keep on asking, and you will receive what you ask for.
Keep on seeking, and you will find.
Keep on knocking, and the door will be opened to you.

---

[14] Linda Winwood, *Mommy, Why Don't We Celebrate Halloween?* (Destiny Image, 2015), 43
[15] 1 Corinthians 10:23
[16] Matthew 16:24
[17] Isaiah 46:9

Divine Exchange

Dear God

Dear Daughter

FALLING TO PIECES

Dear God I'm Desperate

CRYOBANK

Dear God,

My heart aches and my hands quiver as I try to write to You. I'm at a loss for words to describe the nightmare I'm experiencing. My daughter Samantha, 36 years old and divorced, chose to be artificially impregnated with sperm purchased from Fairfax Cryobank. God, what on earth was she thinking? She knows better than to do something so foolish.

Making matters worse, her dad refers to our unborn grandbaby as a bastard. I'm embarrassed—no *ashamed*—to think that my first grandchild's father exists as nothing more than a profile from a catalog. When I drive down Hysteria Lane, neighbors' disapproving stares unnerve me knowing they gossip about this latest development.

God, I'm outraged. I love Samantha, and I know she yearns for motherhood. Paul and I have always been hopeful for her to bear us a grandchild, too, but not through the cold process of a Cryobank.

Oh, dear God, what should I do?

Ann

My Dear Ann,

I see your disappointment and concern over Samantha's decision, and I know your difficult feelings are mixed with anticipation and delight. While you are thrilled for her to become a mother, this scenario isn't the picture you envisioned. Let me help you view these unexpected circumstances from a different perspective.

Samantha, as an *adult*, has made a decision for *her* life. Like you, Ann, she has free will. Some decisions will be excellent. Some options seem plain stupid, and others reflect outright rebellion against Me. The hardest part for you to realize now, whether or not you agree, *her* choice has been made.

Samantha's decision, although painful to both of us, does not change her worth in My sight. Do your decisions, whether right or wrong, change My love for you? Do your choices diminish My character or identity? Certainly not. Likewise, her pregnancy represents no bad reflection on you as her mother. You did as I asked—raised her in the way she should go.[1]

As your neighbors harshly judge you, they reflect weakness in their own character, not yours. You need not cower or feel guilty over decisions made by others. Through this difficult season, I promise to guard your heart.[2]

Paul's lack of sensitivity exasperates you further, and I see how his words cut to your core. You would be wise to speak to him privately in truth and love[3] regarding his hurtful comments. Pray without ceasing,[4] that when he sees the new baby his judgment may soften.

Let me assure you, I know Samantha's every thought, word, and deed.[5] Her choice deviates from My best plan for her life,[6] but she refused to listen to My words and walked in the stubbornness of her own heart.[7] Sadly, she will suffer difficult consequences as a result of her rebellion, because I am just.[8]

Do you think Samantha could have gotten pregnant without My knowledge? Is there anything I don't see?[9] Ann, have you

---

[1] Proverbs 22:6
[2] Philippians 4:6-7
[3] Ephesians 4:15
[4] 1 Thessalonians 5:17
[5] Psalm 139:1-4
[6] Jeremiah 29:11
[7] Kay Arthur, *Lord, I Want to Know You* (CO: Waterbrook Press, 2000), 155
[8] Jeremiah 23:6
[9] Genesis 16:13

forgotten—I AM GOD? In the beginning, I created the heavens and earth,[10] and now I have formed your grandson.[11] Specifically. Thoughtfully. Carefully. I was there when that one particular sperm cell met with Samantha's egg. In that moment, I created a miracle, a living, eternal soul.[12] Not a detail of Joshua's conception, circumstances, or genetics is a mishap to Me.

When your adorable first grandson arrives, he will be exactly as I designed, and you'll be blessed. He has been fearfully and wonderfully made.[13] Like Samantha. Like Edward, the sperm donor, a man I also love. Each represents a miracle created by Me and for Me.[14] So do not let your heart be troubled—trust in Me.[15]

You, dear Grammy, now inherit both new responsibility and privilege. Will you tell Joshua all about Me?[16]

Love,
God

God's Promise: Exodus 14:14

The Lord Himself will fight for you—just stay calm.

---

[10] Genesis 1:1
[11] Colossians 1:16
[12] Kay Arthur, *To Know Him by Name* (Oregon: Multnomah Books, 1995), 13
[13] Psalm 139:14
[14] Colossians 1:16
[15] John 14:1
[16] Joel 1:2-3

Divine Exchange

Dear God

_____

_____

_____

_____

_____

_____

Dear Daughter

_____

_____

_____

_____

_____

_____

GREAT EXPECTATIONS

Dear God,

When I was twelve, my parents divorced. Since then, both Mom and Dad *un*happily *remarried*. I vowed never to have a marriage that resembles the dysfunctional relationships modeled for me growing up.

Now that I'm married, I'm unhappy, too, drifting down the same path toward divorce.

Maybe I expect Todd to be perfect. I guess I expect myself to be perfect, too.

God, I'm desperate for help. How do I avoid making the same mistakes as my parents?

Linda

My Dear Linda,

I am delighted that you have come to me with your concerns in hopes of finding harmony with Todd before it's too late. You have admitted your weaknesses, and I promise to help you.[1] Since I designed marriage for your mutual benefit, when you choose My ways, unity follows. My Word leads you onto a pathway towards fulfillment—in a way you least expect.

---

[1] Psalm 121:2-3

Linda, I never expect you or Todd to be perfect. Each day, My generous grace and forgiveness cover you, drawing you closer to Me and each other.[2] The struggles in your marriage provide a perfect opportunity for you to depend upon Me.[3]

My special daughter, let's take time to reflect upon your expectations for your marriage. Do you strive to serve or be served?[4] What attitudes, behaviors and possessions are you willing to forsake for the benefit of your marriage?[5] Are you expecting Todd to fulfill your needs instead of Me?

The root of your problem lies in the fact that marriage has become your idol taking My rightful place.[6] I AM Almighty God.[7] My strength, protection, and provision surpass that of all men. I did not create Todd to meet all of your needs—that's My role.

As the lover of your soul,[8] intimacy with Me surpasses every other relationship and provides meaning and joy to your life. I am your closest, most trustworthy friend. As your mighty savior, I delight in you with gladness. With My love, I rejoice over you with joyful songs.[9] My direction and wisdom change the trajectory of your relationship with Todd to a God-honoring covenant of Holy matrimony.[10]

To take the first step in the right direction, come to Me each morning on your knees. Acknowledge My sovereignty over every aspect of your life with adoration. Humble yourself and confess your sins. Thank Me for your many blessings, including your hardships, as opportunities to seek Me. Make known all of your needs and the desires of your heart.[11]

---

[2] Ephesians 4:32
[3] 2 Corinthians 12:7a
[4] Galatians 5:13
[5] Romans 12:2
[6] Exodus 20:4
[7] Genesis 17:1
[8] Psalm 23
[9] Zephaniah 3:17
[10] Mark 10:7-9
[11] Acronym ACTS: Serial story by "Marion Harland" (Mary Virginia Terhune) August 8, 1883 publication of the periodical *The Continent*

Next, spend a week fasting—not to deprive you unnecessarily but to eliminate distractions and refocus your priorities. Linda, by giving up Facebook one hour each day and using that time instead to read Psalms. Your undivided attention on Me will deepen our spiritual connection and prepare you to see your marriage through My eyes.

Then, as I provide revelations, forgive Todd. Go to him with a contrite heart and say, *Todd, I was wrong.* Drop your end of the stronghold to end the ongoing tug-of-war that has become a way of life between you. Listen to his point of view and respect his opinions to show your authentic affection.

Communicating in practical ways that Todd understands demonstrates your loving commitment. Rather than disparaging your husband to others, honor him with your words.[12] Choose acts of submission, based on sacrifice rather than control, to express your respect for Todd as the head of your home.[13] As differences arise, always speak truth in love.[14]

Linda, as I watch over you with My tender loving care, you will find hope. With My pure love, you will come to cherish the man I chose for you.

Love,
God

God's Promise: Philippians 4:9

Keep putting into practice all you learned and received from me—then the God of peace will be with you.

---

[12] Proverbs 15:4
[13] Ephesians 5:23
[14] Ephesians 4:15

Divine Exchange

Dear God

_____

_____

_____

_____

_____

_____

Dear Daughter

_____

_____

_____

_____

_____

MOM OF THE DARK AGES

Dear God,

My daughter asked permission to invite Jonathan home for the Thanksgiving holidays. Does this mean she is serious with this boy I've never met? Never stamped with my approval? Melissa's only 26 years old, and that "boyfriend" is certainly no boy. At 29 he's way too old for my baby girl.

God, I'm a nervous wreck over this situation. Too many things could go wrong. What if Jonathan's family is wealthy, and he shuns our humble home? What if I cook a roast, and he's a vegetarian? What if Melissa expects to *sleep* with Jonathan?

I refuse to presume that they sleep together—my Melissa would not do that. Friends laugh at me saying, "Come on, this is not the dark ages. Don't be naïve. They're adults for Pete's sake. Just make up their bed in Melissa's room and forget it. Quit acting like a prude."

I'm trying to do the right thing, but my heart races with every thought of Jonathan. Yet, to tell Melissa that he is not welcome in our home would break her heart.

God, I'm frantic. What should I tell Melissa?

Barbara

My Dear Barbara,

How I hate to see you stress over the details of your life.[1] Allow Me to wash away your fears.[2] Melissa simply wants to share an important person in her life with you. She is not asking for your opinion or moral judgment of Jonathan.

You are wise not to presume they are sexually intimate and wiser still to invite Jonathan to sleep in your designated guest area. It is your responsibility to set boundaries in your home[3] that match your moral convictions and honor My Word.[4]

You will learn much about Jonathan from his reaction[5] to your standard that respects the sanctity of marriage.[6] Your choice will speak of Me without words.[7] Melissa may not agree outwardly with your decision, but she will respect you. Someday she will come to understand that you guarded her heart.[8]

Barbara, why are you frantic to impress Jonathan? I don't want you to miss what is important in My eyes.[9] Will Jonathan's sleep become more peaceful if you buy him designer sheets with a matching down comforter? Will he base his opinion of Melissa on such empty pursuits?

Instead of worrying,[10] remember your gift of hospitality. Why not focus on how to warm Jonathan's heart? What random acts of kindness would help him to feel relaxed and welcomed so you can get to know him?[11] Isn't your time better spent helping Melissa

[1] Matthew 6:25a, 26
[2] Philippians 4:6-9
[3] Psalm 127:1
[4] Psalm 119:1
[5] Proverbs 1:7
[6] 1 Corinthians 7:1
[7] 1 Peter 3:1
[8] Proverbs 4:23
[9] Proverbs 8:6-7
[10] Matthew 6:25
[11] 2 Corinthians 6:6

identify Jonathan's character traits—those lasting marks etched into his soul? How could you extend grace so that Jonathan feels comfortable in your home?

While a house may be beautiful, I treasure a home filled with the fruit of My Spirit.[12] With your gift of hospitality, adorn your home with *love*. Welcome Jonathan with *goodness* from your heart. Toss pillows of *kindness* and *joy*. Drape your windows with a gentle breeze of *peace*. Fill your rooms, no matter the size, with laughter. Keep your words *gentle*.

Barbara, welcome Jonathan into your home because he is important to Melissa. Trust Me by *faith* to watch over you and your family.[13] When you base your choices on My solid foundation, My light shines[14] on each heart and permeates your home with My love.[15]

Love,
God

God's Promise: James 1:5a

If you need wisdom, ask our generous God, and He will give it to you.

---

[12] Galatians 5:22
[13] Psalm 33:18
[14] Psalm 118:27
[15] Psalm 117:2

Divine Exchange

Dear God

_____

_____

_____

_____

_____

Dear Daughter

_____

_____

_____

_____

_____

THE PARENT TRAP

Dear God,

Parenting exasperates me. Constant issues turn our home into a war zone. Ryan and I attempt to serve You as we make decisions for our family,[1] but *gray areas* confuse our thinking. Choices seem impossible, so we argue.

For instance, Ryan and I decided that our children not be allowed to have RoboTripGame[2] until they reach seven years of age—an arbitrary decision. But we needed limits. When our six-year old entrepreneur, Nicholas, announced he planned to earn money to buy the game, we smiled at his ingenuity.

Then he implemented his plan. He asked for extra chores and saved all the money he earned. He stashed gifts of cash from Gramps along with every penny he found on the ground. Now, Nicholas has saved $84 and has asked to shop for his RoboTripGame.

What do we do?

If Ryan and I refuse to allow Nicholas to spend the money he saved, he gets punished for his success. That seems wrong, because we want him to develop a strong work ethic. If we say *yes* to his purchase of RoboTripGame at age six, we disregard our rule intended to protect his best interests in the long run.

---

[1] Joshua 24:15b

[2] http://www.webmd.com/parenting/features/teen-drug-slang-dictionary-for-parents#2. Note: The name of this game was chosen to alert parents to the subtle, destructive messages prevalent in our culture.

God, I feel overwhelmed in uncharted territory. How do I survive parenting without losing my mind?

Amber

My Dear Amber,

As you have expressed, parenting stretches your patience and faith beyond measure. Like a salmon swimming upstream, you face constant currents rushing against you. I commend you for your endurance,[3] and I have a plan to help you.

Around the second bend on Hysteria Lane lives a delightful couple mature in their faith.[4] Joe and Carolyn Gordon fought the good fight[5] of parenting, and they are eager to mentor a young couple.[6] Their experiences will help you apply My Word to everyday situations, and they will encourage you along your parenting journey. In turn, your family will bless their lives.

As you face difficult choices, they will counsel you in My Truth.[7] With their guidance, you will understand My important principles underpinning rules you implement. They will provide you with insights from Me to help you understand the long-term impact of family patterns developed during these early years.[8] They will cover you with persistent prayer.[9] I have arranged for you to meet.

Now, about Nicholas—praise him for his hard work. Then, encourage him with your commitment to shop for an appropriate gift, instead of RoboTripGame, to celebrate his birthday. In the

---

[3] Romans 5:4
[4] Ephesians 4:12-13
[5] 1 Timothy 1:18
[6] Titus 2:4-8
[7] Job 12:12-13
[8] Proverbs 1:4-7; 2:1-11; 3:5-6
[9] Ephesians 6:18

meantime, there are valuable lessons for your ingenious son to learn.

Consider the principles you want to teach Nicholas to develop his character. For instance, does he tithe?[10] To help him develop a spirit of generosity and compassion, could he share the fruit of his hard work with someone else less fortunate?[11] Has he mastered the concept of delayed gratification?[12] Have you instilled in him an attitude of gratitude?[13]

Lessons you teach Nicholas as a child become the principles by which he governs his priorities in the future.[14] Discipline Nicholas while there is still hope, lest you ruin his life.[15] Choose gentle words mindful to not exasperate him[16] or crush his tender spirit.[17] Consistency, the most difficult aspect of parenting, produces success, so when you say "no," mean no.[18]

My precious Amber, I have entrusted you and Ryan to parent Nicholas. Teach him My ways, and build your home on the solid rock of My Word.[19] Because you surely reap what you sow, stand firm and confident in My strength as you parent on your knees.

Love,
God

God's Promise: Proverbs 22:6

Direct your children onto the right path, and when they are older, they will not leave it.

---

[10] Malachi 3:10
[11] Proverbs 3:9
[12] Genesis 25:29-34
[13] Psalm 47:1-2
[14] Proverbs 22:6
[15] Proverbs19:18
[16] Ephesians 6:4a
[17] Proverbs 15:4
[18] Matthew 5:37
[19] Luke 6:48

Divine Exchange

Dear God

_____

_____

_____

_____

_____

Dear Daughter

_____

_____

_____

_____

_____

THE WORST PERSON I KNOW

Dear God,

Margaret—the worst person I know. I've tried everything to get along with my mother-in-law, but how? When she barges into our home unannounced, tension grips my entire body. That woman invites herself to dinner and grumbles throughout the meal. She rearranges our furniture at will. And to top it all off, she complains about how we raise the kids. As soon as she leaves, my frazzled nerves snap at my husband.

Randy expresses frustration, too. Yet, he takes no action to stop his mother's rankling antics. While I rage, he simply says, "Honey, be patient. She doesn't mean any harm."

God, I'm desperate. What can I do about my meddling mother-in-law?

Alison

My Dear Alison,

I know Margaret exasperates you, and I see the tension she causes with Randy. I've known Margaret for over 63 years, and indeed she is a *strong* woman. Since she may live for many more years, you must work to reconcile your relationship[1] by making different choices.

Your first thought is to change Margaret, but you can't change others. Since you have no control over her behavior, she'll continue to annoy you. You could continue the same frustrating, destructive cycle, and watch your marriage continue to erode, but

---

[1] Matthew 5:24b

that seems foolish. You also secretly considered another option to relieve the tension in your home—separation. You know how I feel about divorce,[2] and breaking your vow to Randy will devastate your entire family. Before you resort to drastic measures, will you pause a moment and let Me help you examine your own heart?

Do you listen to Margaret with compassion? Do you choose words to affirm her positive character traits? Are you kind and patient when you speak? Are you willing to surrender your pride and allow Me to change your attitude[3] toward her?

You cringe at My words, and I know your thoughts.[4] *God, that's not fair, it's not my fault. It's Margaret's fault.*

Your angry emotions stir, and your heels dig in to stand firm on the position that you are *right*. However, my thoughts are nothing like your thoughts. My ways are far beyond anything you could imagine.[5]

Alison, when you are ready to trust Me regarding Margaret, I will help you.[6] To restore harmony in your home, *you* must make a decision to honestly face your part in the problem rather than blame her. Are you willing to admit your own sins[7] and allow My Word to transform your thoughts[8] toward Margaret?

To rebuild unity in your family, you must learn to speak truth in *love*.[9] First talk with Randy privately, and be tenderhearted toward him.[10] Then, together decide how to approach Margaret with patience, kindness, love, and good intentions.[11] Remain strong and united in your purpose to reconcile.[12]

---

[2] Malachi 2:16
[3] Jeremiah 4:4
[4] Psalm 94:11
[5] Isaiah 55:8
[6] Psalm 28:7
[7] 1 John 1:8-9
[8] Romans 12:2
[9] Ephesians 4:15
[10] 1 Peter 3:8
[11] Galatians 5:22
[12] 1 Corinthians 1:10

Over time, if you see no evidence of progress, don't lose heart in doing good.[13] Instead, continue to support Margaret according to *her* needs and benefit.[14] Be kind and forgiving.[15] No matter how difficult Margaret becomes, do not let any unwholesome talk come out of your mouth.[16] Do not let the sun set on your anger. Instead, tell Me your difficult feelings. Then I will comfort you and have compassion for you.[17]

These things I ask of you, Alison, seem difficult. But, I am your God, and I will strengthen you and help you.[18] I promise to sustain you[19] through these difficult times with My constant tender-loving care. Hold firm to the truth that nothing is impossible with Me by your side.[20] As you consistently sow love into Margaret's life, in My timing you will reap blessings in return.[21]

Remember, My dear Alison, not even Margaret can separate you from My love.[22]

Love,
God

God's Promise: Psalm 32:8

I will guide you along the best pathway for your life.
I will advise you and watch over you.

---

[13] Galatians 6:9
[14] Ephesians 4:29b
[15] Ephesians 4:32
[16] Ephesians 4:29a
[17] Isaiah 49:13
[18] Isaiah 41:10
[19] Psalm 55:22
[20] Luke 1:37
[21] Galatians 6:9
[22] Romans 8:38-39

Divine Exchange

Dear God

_____

_____

_____

_____

_____

Dear Daughter

_____

_____

_____

_____

_____

Jeanne LeMay

WON'T YOU BE MY NEIGHBOR?

Dear God,

Last year a wonderful, friendly young couple moved to Hysteria Lane. They care for their property, serve families in the neighborhood by baby-sitting on weekends, and never cause problems. We have grown to treasure their friendship.

My concern is that Adam and Bob are homosexual. In church, the pastor said that gays are rejected by You. On the news, a broadcaster reported that a large, local congregation had split apart over this issue that caused controversy and strife.

God, I'm confused. If you are the loving God You claim to be, how can You condemn my thoughtful, sensitive neighbors?

Mary

My Dear Mary,

How wise for you to love your neighbors.[1] As you examine your beliefs in the context of today's culture, I understand your confusion. To answer difficult questions about your daily life, My Word teaches you what is true and helps you discern right from wrong.[2] What I have spoken to you proclaims absolute Truth and sheds My light on this situation.

---

[1] Matthew 22:39
[2] 2 Timothy 3:16

Did I not create you *and* your neighbors in My image, special in My sight?[3] Because I treasure each of you and long to protect you, I established the covenant of marriage as the union between one man and one woman.[4] When anyone rejects Me by deviating from My original plan, My heart grieves.

Adam and Bob are precious to Me. I allow them free will to live as they choose—trapped in a downward spiral of sin. Yet, because I am Holy, I cannot condone their immoral behavior. Nor should you approve of sin. My precious Mary, please do not be deceived[5] by political correctness—destructive consequences always follow transgressions.

Choosing *any* rebellious lifestyle, including gossip on Hysteria Lane as well as homosexuality, causes separation from Me.[6] However, there is hope for everyone, because My Word serves as the perfect guide to love, joy, and peace. When my lost children come to Me by faith with honest humility, acknowledge their sins and turn from them, they receive My mercy.[7]

When Adam and Bob readily admit their mistake, I am here to forgive them and promise to remove their guilt and shame as far as the east is from west.[8]

In the meantime, why not bless them with random acts of kindness? Comfort them in sadness. Invite them to church. Pray for them to turn their hearts and lives toward Me. Mary, will you love them on My behalf so your actions *and attitude* proclaim My glory?

Love,
God

---

[3] Genesis 1:27
[4] Genesis 2:18-25
[5] 1 Corinthians 6:9-10
[6] Proverbs 5:21-23
[7] Proverbs 28:13b
[8] Psalm 103:2-5;11-13.

God's Promise: Romans 4:7

> Oh, what joy for those whose disobedience is forgiven
> whose sins are put out of sight.

Divine Exchange

Dear God

_____

_____

_____

_____

_____

_____

Dear Daughter

_____

_____

_____

_____

_____

Jeanne LeMay

PUT ON A HAPPY FACE

Dear God I'm Desperate

BUSHWHACKED

Dear God,

The Whites' win the "Entertainers of the Year" Grammy Award on Hysteria Lane. Once a month, residents receive an engraved invitation for an event unmatched by Martha Stewart. When ours arrived, I couldn't wait to shop for a new little black dress.

Approaching the White's home, Robert appeared as handsome in his tuxedo as he looked on our wedding day. My confidence level spiked to ten. As we strolled up the manicured walkway and ascended the marble staircase, we were greeted by the scent of fresh flowers from their custom-designed wreath.

Comparing the White's magnificent property pricked my confidence as I reflected on our front door with its makeshift plastic wreath purchased at JoAnn's "after Christmas sale" last year.

As her butler welcomed us into the exquisite foyer with its grand staircase, I remembered my own smaller entryway, and my confidence dropped from ten to nine. With the aroma of Gwyneth's cooking of recipes from Southern Living Magazine, I compared my lack of culinary skills to hers, and my confidence dipped to eight.

When Mr. and Mrs. Marcus J. White, III greeted us in their Neiman Marcus finery, I sulked in my new dress from T. J. Maxx. As we began to mingle with the White's prestigious guests, I felt scrutinized by their stares and unimportant when measured against their credentials. My heart deflated.

When the clock struck midnight, I fled down the boxwood-lined pathway and swore to Robert I'd never go back to the White's house again as long as I lived.

God, I don't know what happens to me during those evenings. I feel inferior and bushwhacked.

Misty

My Dear Misty,

How disappointing for you to anticipate an enjoyable evening and then falter because of the White's opulence. Truly, they possess worldly advantages and possessions greater than yours, and comparing is only natural. How disparaging to expect kind greetings from neighbors and instead find yourself bushwhacked by condemning glances. With their own faults wrapped in beautiful clothing, their subtle sniping pierced your spirit and heart. No wonder you felt vulnerable and undone.

So often you allow opinions of others to trap your heart. Then your own thoughts or feelings about yourself condemn your value. When you believe these things and live accordingly, you're held captive by very real but invisible misconceptions.[1]

Have you forgotten *whose* you are? I have chosen you from many, and adopted you as My own child.[2] You are My beloved daughter, Heir to My kingdom with riches untold. I set you apart from all others for Myself.[3]

My precious daughter, will you look into the reflection of My eyes and see yourself as I see you? To Me you are blameless, and I delight in revealing the deep secrets of My heart to you.[4] You are

[1] Kay Arthur, *Free From Bondage God's Way*, (OR: Harvest House Publishers, 1994), 50
[2] Ephesians 1:4-5
[3] Psalm 4:3
[4] 1 Corinthians 2:10

blessed with My wisdom more precious than rubies; nothing you desire of your neighbors can compare.[5] In fact, you are so special I marked you with a sacred seal—My Holy Spirit.

Misty, the next time you enter the White's home, please don't judge yourself as inferior. Instead, hold your head high with confidence, for you are a crown of splendor, a royal diadem, in My hand.[6] Listen to the trumpets of heaven announce your arrival. Let bystanders marvel at your attire, for you are adorned with a garland of My grace and display a necklace of My wisdom.[7] With My Spirit of peace etched within your heart, your face glows with My love.[8] Nothing of this world compares to your stature. My daughter, you are secure in My everlasting love.

Love,
God

God's Promise: Psalm 139:17

> How precious are your thoughts about me, O God.
> They cannot be numbered!

---

[5] Proverbs 3:15
[6] Isaiah 62:3
[7] Proverbs 1:1-9
[8] Luke 11:35

Divine Exchange

Dear God

_____

_____

_____

_____

_____

Dear Daughter

_____

_____

_____

_____

_____

I'M A MESS!

Dear God,

My whole life I've been quite a handful for You—what sin have I not committed?[1] My tormented mind reels with guilt over all my bad choices. I deceived myself into thinking no one would ever discover my secret life.

Then today, all of a sudden, I realized that *YOU* saw my every selfish, manipulating deed. You knew my bitter thoughts, hidden resentments, and harsh judgments against others and myself as they took root in my heart. You watched as I slept with one man after another. You agonized over my lie to Jay that he fathered my baby so he would marry me.

As I reflect on my shameful life, I feel dirty, because *You eye-witnessed everything.*[2]

The Bible says that You care about people when they're a total wreck. But how could those words apply to me? How could You possibly still love me after all I've done wrong? How could *anyone* ever love me again?

God, help. My life's a mess.

Julie

My Dear Julie,

I have watched from afar as you stumbled through the Valley of Trouble.[3] My heart ached the second you rejected My love for

---

[1] Psalm 25:17
[2] Psalm 11:4
[3] Psalm 23:4

you. My teardrops mingled with yours every moment of every day. All these years, in silence I have waited to hold you in My arms again and lavish you with My love.[4]

Julie, you have chosen to live carelessly outside of My best desires for you. Sadly, as a result, you now suffer pain and shame. Yet, those unwise decisions never diminished your value to Me. I never rejected you. No matter what you've done, my precious daughter, how could I possibly turn My back on you?

I see you now, trembling, broken and spent as you cry to Me for help. I know, deep in your heart, you lament the wasted years of your life. Since you now admit your sins and return to Me with your whole heart, I'll wipe your slate clean and give you a fresh start. [5] I promise to act on your behalf and help you turn your life around in My perfect way and timing.

I love you, my daughter, with My everlasting love. With My unfailing love, I draw you close to My heart.[6] Take My kind and gentle hand now, and I'll shelter you in the shadow of My wings.[7] I'll lead you to a fulfilling life with hope for your future.[8]

Julie, I forgive you.

I forgive you.

I forgive you.[9]

Love,
God

God's Promise: Psalm 32:5

> Finally I confessed all my sins to you and stopped trying to hide my guilt. And you forgave me! All my guilt is gone!

---

[4] Psalm 31:18
[5] Psalm 32:5b
[6] Jeremiah 31:3
[7] Psalm 36:7
[8] Jeremiah 29:11
[9] Luke 7:47-48

Divine Exchange

Dear God

_____

_____

_____

_____

_____

_____

Dear Daughter

_____

_____

_____

_____

_____

JASON'S GREEN BERET

Dear God,

Tonight's one of those nights I hate. Because of news reports on TV, there's a heightened sense of tension and disrespect about the war, and I feel faint-hearted for my groom. Within a month after our wedding, he deployed to Afghanistan.

To hasten the 8,760-minute wait until our sweet reunion, I attend nursing school. Long days at the clinic, bathing eighty-year-old women and changing their diapers, leave me no time to fret about Jason.

When I get home, Tramp and Lady greet me with their wagging tails as they slobber me with kisses. That's how the three of us begin our evening routine. Then we wait for a tender moment by phone with "daddy." If he calls, I'm relieved—he's safe another day. Lonely with only my puppies, I crawl in bed. Exhausted, I hope to sleep.

But not tonight.

Depression leaves me forlorn like the old woman alone at the clinic forgotten by her family. Or a widow who passes long hours looking at the street. Who can understand the life of my faithful Green Beret serving his country? Who can understand the longing and waiting and wondering of his wife?

Without Jason, my imagination plays nasty tricks. In my mind's eye, through the mist, a shiny black military vehicle parks in our driveway. A distinguished officer soon comes into view— his furrowed brow reveals his mission. The click of his spit-shined shoes on the brick sidewalk breaks the endless silence of the night.

Is that protocol? I don't know. I dare not ask. For my question may bring dread to my doorstep.

God, how long must I wrestle with my thoughts and hide agony in my solitary heart?

I miss the scent of Jason's skin after he showered. His caress when he stroked my hair. Laughter in his eyes after he teased. The taste of his favorite peppermint candy as the flavor lingered on his lips. His gentle voice when he whispered my name. Warmth from his body snuggled close to mine.

I lie awake like a bird alone on a metal roof. The bedroom walls press me in with fears from all corners. God, I am so lonesome I could die. How do I cope with this hole in my heart?

Leah

My Dear Leah,

You are a courageous woman to shoulder the heart of a soldier. Your compassion for others is true to My own heart.[1] While you are separated by war from the man you love, your burdens are many. Few understand your plight. Leah, although you appear to be brave for Jason's sake, I know your deepest secret— you feel vulnerable.

I know everything about you, spring bride. I know every fear. And I promise to protect you and keep you safe.[2] You may feel lonely, but you are never alone. Although you can't see Me, I am always with you.[3] I tend to you like your maid of honor, who cared for your needs on your wedding day.[4] You are always on my mind and never separated from My love.[5]

---

[1] Psalm 145:9
[2] Psalm 91:4-6
[3] Psalm 9:10
[4] Psalm 23:1
[5] Romans 8:39

Come, My precious bride. Come to My open arms. When your heart aches, whisper My name. When you feel uneasy, let Me caress you with My gentle Spirit. Bring each burden to Me, and you will find rest for your soul.[6]

Allow My light to shine upon your face,[7] and then even the darkness will not seem dark.[8] Taste My wine to gladden your heart.[9] Feast on My bread of life, and you will see that I am always good.[10] Your soul will be satisfied as with the richest of foods.[11] Just as Jason's fragrance gives you delight, a sweet friendship with Me will refresh your soul[12] and fill the air with an aroma redolent with life.[13]

Leah, these promises I wrote for you and Jason long before you were born. Engrave them in your heart, for they will be life to you as you grasp them.[14]

I am the stronghold of your life. Who shall you fear?
For I, the Lord, shield you. When you cry to Me, I answer.
When evil men advance against you, they will stumble and
fall.[15]

Though an army besieges you, your hearts need not fear.
Though war breaks out against you, even then be
confident. For in the day of trouble, I will keep you safe.
You will lie down and sleep in peace.[16]

---

[6] Matthew 11:28-29
[7] Psalm 31:16
[8] Psalm 139:12
[9] Psalm 104:15
[10] Psalm 34:8
[11] Psalm 63:5
[12] Proverb 27:9 (Message)
[13] 2 Corinthians 2:14 (Message)
[14] Proverb 4:21-22
[15] Psalm 3:3-4; 27:1-2
[16] Psalm 27:3, 5; 4:8a

Your enemies will turn back when you call on Me for help. By this you will know that I am God.
When you feel afraid, trust Me. I am your refuge and fortress.[17]

Do not fear the terror of night, nor the missiles that fly by day, for My faithfulness is your shield and rampart.
If you make Me your refuge, though a thousand may fall at your side, no harm will befall you. No disaster will come near your tent.[18]

Because you love Me, I will rescue you.
I will command My angels to post guard over you.
Because you acknowledge Me as your Lord and Savior,
I will answer when you call on Me and show you My salvation.[19]

Love,
God

God's Promise: Joshua 1:5

No one will be able to stand against you. As I was with Moses, so I will be with you. I will never leave you or forsake you.

---

[17] Psalm 56:4, 9; 91:2
[18] Psalm 91:4-5, 7-10
[19] Psalm 91:14-16

Divine Exchange

Dear God

_____

_____

_____

_____

_____

_____

Dear Daughter

_____

_____

_____

_____

_____

SPEAK NO EVIL

Dear God,

Intuitively I knew, but scary thoughts spiked my anxiety. If I speak the C-word, will it spread into my future? As fear metastasized throughout my body, I swallowed the lump in my throat, and dragged my weary self to the sterile medical center.

Dr. Webster efficiently and methodically proceeded with the exam and avoided eye contact. My hands trembled and goose bumps covered my arms as terror crept into my heart.

The C-word was not mentioned.

"Who is your surgeon?" She asked.

As she continued talking, somewhere in my subconscious I knew Dr. Webster conveyed important information, but my comprehension quickly deteriorated.

"Go straight to Dr. Mason . . . I'm forwarding your records and an updated prescription for further tests. He'll see you this afternoon."

My emotions raced like wildfire. Oh my God, no. I can't possibly have c . . . c . . . ca . . .

Why me? What do I do now?

Sally

My Dear Sally,

Come into Daddy's arms.[1] I know you feel naked and vulnerable in your hospital gown. I'm waiting to hold you. I know the width and breadth of your fears, and I won't leave you alone, so don't be afraid.[2] Will you be brave while I hold your heart close to Mine?

Sally, you will find rest for your soul when your hope is in Me. With unmistakable clarity, you will sense My presence, even in the midst of the unbearable struggles ahead.[3] I will not let your hopes be crushed,[4] because I have a future planned especially for you. I will sustain you as I have promised. You will know I am the Lord, and you will not be disappointed[5] even in your suffering. Cling to your hope in Me, the firm and secure anchor of your soul.[6]

In your isolation at the hospital, I will deepen your awareness of My presence. Pour out your heart bringing your anguish to Me. As you share your cries of desperation, I will reveal My heart and deepest secrets to you. Allow Me to become the rock-solid center of your life. Choose to trust My heart of love. Then, you will sense stability at your core, and you will never feel alone.[7]

Sally, run to Daddy. Trust Me more, letting go of your control and expectations in order to make room for My grace in all it's amazing forms. Breathe in My grace, and breathe out your praise as I wrap you in My blanket of love.[8] Despite your doubts and fears. I will take care of you. Grasp My perfect love for you, because there is nothing that can separate you from My love.[9]

---

[1] Romans 8:14-16
[2] Matthew 10:30
[3] Sandra D. Wilson, Ph.D. & Larry Crabb. *Into Abba's Arms: Finding the Acceptance You've Always Wanted* (IL: Tyndale House Publishers, 1998), 155
[4] Psalm 119:114, 116
[5] Isaiah 49:23e
[6] Hebrews 6:19
[7] Ibid. 30-41, 64
[8] Elaine Greydanus Bush, *Three Generations Fight Cancer Together: Lessons Learned on the Journey*, Central FL: EA Books Publishing, 2017, 21, 71

Through your struggle, you will experience peace cradled in My arms.

Love,
God

God's Promise: 1 Peter 4:19

>If you are suffering in a manner that pleases God, keep on doing what is right and trust your life to God who created you, for he will never fail you.

.

---

[9] Romans 8:38-39

Divine Exchange

Dear God

_____

_____

_____

_____

_____

_____

Dear Daughter

_____

_____

_____

_____

_____

_____

LOSER-MAGNET

Dear God,

No matter who wears the pants in my life—Jack or Brian or Bill or Max—the pattern repeats. A handsome, eligible, talkative man attracts my attention. He seems so incredible that I can't believe he takes an interest in me. Soon, he boasts his way into my heart.

That's how my exciting relationship began with Michael. But, after four months and eight days from our first date, I noticed that he dominated every conversation and addressed me in a hectoring, self-important manner without listening to my point of view. Yet, I continued to share my heart.

We've been dating over two years now, and he's become more and more brusque. I withdraw and hide my feelings to prevent his anger. He constantly lies, but I remain loyal and believe he will give an honest answer the next time.

For example, yesterday Michael called, "Susan, I have a surprise for you. I'll pick you up for dinner at six o'clock. I love you." Click.

Excitement stirred my emotions as I checked my watch for the umpteenth time. *Where is Michael?* I noticed sweat on my blouse as I paced. Six forty eight. Six fifty nine. Seven thirty one. I held my head tall and reassured myself that everything would be fine. *Why am I getting upset? Something must have happened, or he would be here. I know he loves me—he just told me on the phone.* My brow tightened. I felt like Charlie Brown counting on Lucy as tears smeared mascara across my pillow.

The next day, I called Michael.

"Oh hi Susie, honey. No, nothing bad happened. Why do you ask? I just dozed watching the Packers romp the Bears. You shoulda seen Farve fire those touchdown passes. He was hot. The Bears got creamed, and they deserved it. What? Can't we just go tonight instead? I'll pick you up at six sharp. Susan, yes, I promise. Yes, I still love you. Why wouldn't I?"

Six o'clock. Again, no Michael. Six ten. Six thirteen.

Finally, at 6:45 Michael called. "Hi Susie-Q. I've only got a minute—and one phone call. The cop pulled me over. I didn't deserve it. Anyway, can you come? How soon can you get here? There was a fight, too. Will you bring my Packers hat? I left it by the couch. See you in a few. Oh, by the way, I love you."

Sitting in the police station was not unfamiliar. The old, dingy building felt dismal and smelled like sweat. When Michael greeted me, his sandpaper beard scraped my cheek, and his breath confirmed my worst fears.

God, Michael has a drinking problem. Just like Jack. And Brian. And all the others.

Again, I gave too much of myself to a dead-end relationship. Again, I'm in too deep to turn back. Everybody loves Michael. They wouldn't believe anything negative about him. Besides, he promised he would get counseling after we get married. Then everything will be fine.

When I look in the mirror, I see sad eyes with circles beneath too dark to conceal. With Michael, like all the men before him, I never laugh anymore. The tension hangs between us like heavy smog. When I allow myself to feel, I'm nervous and angry.

God, it's my fault. I expect too much of Michael. I can't do anything right—not even love.

Susie

My Dear Susie,

Draw near to Me, my beloved daughter.[1] You have endured endless pain from unreliable men. No wonder you feel angry and confused. Bombarded with double messages,[2] you have been robbed of peace.

I love you, but not enough to tell the truth.

I love you, but not enough to keep my promises.

I don't have a drinking problem, but I'll get help when we get married.

From alcoholic parents, you inherited many distorted attitudes and beliefs, just like you inherited those beautiful brown eyes. Sadly, you are left with consequences of your family's inappropriate, addictive behaviors from the third and fourth generations.[3] Do you not remember all the secrets and lies harbored by your parents growing up?

"But Mom, Dad promised to pick me up today."

"I know Dad promised, Susan, but he's sick. He can't help it. It would really help me if you walk. You know not to tell Mrs. Simmons that Dad came home from work sick again, right?"

No wonder you have difficulty with intimate relationships—you must *guess* at what is normal.[4]

Just like you longed for approval and affirmation from your dad, you long for love from an addict who is not capable of a mature, loving relationship. When you become disappointed with the inevitable, you overreact and assume responsibility for every problem in order to keep peace. No wonder you are exhausted with circles under those beautiful brown eyes.

---

[1] James 4:8
[2] Janet G. Woititz, Ed.D., *Adult Children of Alcoholics* (FL: Health Communications, Inc., 1983), 19
[3] Exodus 34:7
[4] Janet G. Woititz, Ed.D. 24, 68

You remain loyal to the men who destroy your heart, while you judge yourself without mercy. Over and over you lock yourself into difficult relationships without giving serious consideration to alternatives or consequences. This impulsivity leads to confusion and self-loathing.[5] Indeed, you became a victim from the generational sin of alcoholism.

Susie, don't despair—I bring you good news. When you are caught in a dysfunctional relationship, I will help you escape like a bird from a hunter's trap.[6] Keep your beautiful, sad eyes on Me, and hold My hand. I will help you untwist the love-knots that tangle your life as you discover My foolproof plan in My Word.

The Holy Bible is the greatest book on recovery ever written. It records how the world began and how I created it to be good. Then it tells about the beginning of sin—the first time people decided to reject My plan. The Bible spells out the fatal consequences that result from rejecting My program. However, you will not be left in despair, for when you follow My instructions, you will learn healthy ways to relate to others as I heal your wounded soul.[7]

My precious, daughter, turn your eyes away from worthless things, and I will preserve your life.[8] It is time to leave your repeated failures and disappointing relationships behind. On a path to spiritual wholeness, your broken heart will be healed, and the beautiful dreams I planted within your soul can become reality.

Trust in Me alone, Susie. I will build you up, not tear you down. For I love you with unconditional, everlasting love. You are priceless.

Love,
God

---

[5] Janet G. Woititz, Ed.D. 77, 81, 64, 86, 90
[6] Psalm 124:7-8
[7] Life Recovery Bible (IL: Tyndale House Publishers, Inc., 1998), Preface
[8] Psalm 119:37

God's Promise: Ephesians 1:4
Even before He made the world, God loved us and chose us to be holy and without fault in His eyes.

Divine Exchange

Dear God

_____

_____

_____

_____

_____

Dear Daughter

_____

_____

_____

_____

_____

WORRY, WORRY, WORRY WART

Dear God,

Worry about everything torments my mind twenty-four-seven. If situations don't go well, I feel anxious. If circumstances seem perfect, I fear they will change. I worry about what other people could, might or don't do. I worry about what people think of me or that they don't bother to think of me at all.

I worry about too much work, lack of work, losing work, not wanting to work, stress of work, or not enough money from work. Deadlines kill me. Money stresses me. Anxiety drains me. I need tranquilizers, sleeping pills or cocktails to cope.

God, now I'm worried that I'm too worried. How do I find peace of mind?

Anna

My Dear Anna,

I empathize with your panic and fears and see your depleted spirit. In this fast-paced, faithless world, worry has become the status quo. You have come to the right One for advice—I offer you a foolproof, time-tested solution for eliminating worry.

Anna, I tell you, don't worry. Again I say, do not be anxious about anything,[1] for I am in control of everything.[2]

---

[1] Philippians 4:6
[2] Psalm 97:9

I know what you're thinking. *That's it? Your remedy is to quit worrying? How? You're kidding, right? With my life? Impossible.*

Have you forgotten that I know every detail of your life, and I will guide you[3] as you replace every worry with prayer. Pray about everything.[4]

Again, I know your thoughts. *God, you must be kidding—I have no idea how to pray. What would I say? What will my friends think when they hear this outrageous plan? I don't have time.*

My dear child, you have a choice. You can continue to worry endlessly and rely on your own depleted strength, or you can pray without ceasing[5] and receive My unlimited help and eventually find true peace. Let me explain.

Share your every thought with Me. When you kneel in prayer and empty your heart, I hear and respond. Listen for My answer amidst the noise of this world. In My still small voice, I may give you direction and wisdom or nudge your conscience. I may ask you to wait to make a decision or prompt you to forgive someone who hurt you.

My advice is always wise,[6] because I know every unseen detail of every situation. From me no secrets are hidden.[7] Each new day, I equip you with a perfect plan, so you can prioritize and make choices with confidence. No more second-guessing. When you come to Me with your whole heart, I give your soul rest.[8]

As you consider your choice to fret or trust Me, Anna, will you take a moment to ponder every good thing in your life? Remember the warmth of the sun on your skin. The sound of your children's laughter. Your husband sharing secrets over coffee. Nothing is too small to appreciate, and all good things come from Me.

---

[3] Psalm 25:9
[4] Philippians 4:6
[5] Ephesians 6:18
[6] Proverbs 2:6
[7] Matthew 6:18
[8] Matthew 11:29

Instead of focusing on circumstances that create angst, fix your thoughts on what is true, honorable, and right, and pure, and lovely, and admirable. Think about things that are excellent and worthy of praise.[9]

As you begin to practice humbling yourself before Me with an attitude of gratitude, you will experience My peace in the midst of *all* circumstances.[10] I promise.

Love,
God

God's Promise: Matthew 11:28

> Come to me, all of you who are weary and carry heavy burdens, and I will give you rest.

---

[9] Philippians 4:8-9
[10] Philippians 4:7

Divine Exchange

Dear God

_____

_____

_____

_____

_____

_____

Dear Daughter

_____

_____

_____

_____

_____

_____

RAIN ON MY PARADE

Dear God I'm Desperate

BLUE CHRISTMAS

Dear God,

I hate holidays.

When I think of celebrating, sadness wraps around me like a heavy, drab coat. Commercials show sleigh rides and singing choirs, but my home has always been filled with arguing, complaining, and drunken relatives. Christmas joy remains an elusive dream about a happy family joined together by loving hearts for a meal of turkey with all the trimmings.

Instead, endless difficulties dash my hopes. Why separation? Where do I hide from the mounting pile of bills? How do I make sense of my fragmented life?

In the midst of all this chaos, I want to scream, "Why doesn't anybody care?"

This holiday season, instead of love and laughter, dreadful hollow days and lonely nights await. Christmas Eve I'll sit home alone with a peanut butter sandwich on stale bread.

God, with all my hope lost,[1] how do I survive the holidays?

Elizabeth

My Dear Elizabeth,

I hear you.[2] Every difficult emotion and disappointment you expressed concerns Me.[3] Now that you realize your need for Me, the Kingdom of Heaven is yours.[4]

---

[1] Psalm 6:2-3
[2] Psalm 34:15
[3] Psalm 55:17

The depth of your sorrow as Christmas approaches stirs My compassion.[5] Each holiday as you suffered, My heart broke, too. Your dysfunctional family behaved worlds apart from My intentions.[6] But don't lose heart, My precious one.[7] As you mourn your fragmented life, I am here to comfort you and provide for your needs. I will lead you to peaceful streams and renew your strength. I promise to protect you and guide you along a new path until your life overflows with blessings.[8]

Just as I spoke meaning into emptiness when I created the world,[9] I'm eager to transform your life into a purposeful journey.[10] If you would like to put aside all that has passed, be refreshed, and find hope, then I have the perfect Christmas present for you.[11] It's tucked into a true story written by a doctor named Luke.[12] Curl up by Me now as I share with you—My heart to yours.

"Once upon a time, long, long, ago, I sent My angel Gabriel to visit a young woman named Mary, who was engaged to a man named Joseph.

"The angel spoke to Mary, 'Greetings to you highly favored woman. The Lord is with you.'

"Mary, startled by the visitation, wondered what the angel meant.

"Gabriel said, 'Do not be afraid, Mary, for you have found favor with God. You will conceive and give birth to a son. You will name him Jesus, 'the Lord saves.' Jesus will be very great among men and shall be called 'Son of the Most High,' for the Lord God will give him the throne

---

[4] Matthew 5:3-4
[5] Isaiah 30:18
[6] Psalm 33:11
[7] Psalm 42:5a
[8] Psalm 23
[9] Genesis 1:1-3
[10] Colossians 2:6
[11] John 4:10
[12] Luke 1:26-40

of his Father. He will reign forever, and his kingdom will never end.'

"Mary, confused by the words spoken by the angel, asked, 'How could this happen since I am a virgin?'

"Gabriel answered, 'The Holy Spirit will come upon you, and the power of God Almighty will overshadow you. The Holy One to be born will be called the Son of God. For nothing is impossible with God.'

"Mary said, 'I am the Lord's servant. May it be as you say.'

"Then the angel left Mary to her own thoughts as she praised the Lord.

"So it came to pass, during the third trimester of Mary's pregnancy, Joseph took her to Bethlehem to register for a census required by the laws of those times. While they were there, the time came for the baby to be born, and she gave birth to her firstborn, a son, and they named him Jesus."

Elizabeth, this story reveals the mystery of Christmas.[13] Now, like Mary, you are probably wondering, *why is God telling me this? How does the birth of a baby named Jesus relate to my holiday stress?*

The truth is, these events occurred to restore your relationship with Me.[14] Jesus was born fully human to a woman named Mary, conceived by Me, God Almighty.[15] He grew into a man who was pure, without sin.[16] My precious child, Jesus' birth marks the day I came from heaven to earth for *you*.[17]

Jesus—My gift to you.[18]

---

[13] John 3:16, 31-36
[14] John 14:6
[15] Luke 1:26-37
[16] 1 John 3:5
[17] John 1:13-14; 3:3-7, 15
[18] John 4:10

When you accept this truth, I'll reveal to you a new lifestyle[19] filled with love, security, and significance. I AM calling your name. Do you hear My still small voice in your heart?[20] If you are willing to take My hand and walk into your future with Me, I will guide you to a purposeful life.[21]

Elizabeth, My most important question for you—will you accept my gift?[22]

Love,
God

God's Promise: Romans 4:16

Eternal life is received by faith—given as a free gift.

---

[19] 2 Corinthians 3:6; 5:17
[20] John 10:14-16
[21] Psalm 23
[22] Matthew 16:15-16

Jeanne LeMay

Divine Exchange

Dear God

Dear Daughter

I HATE MY LIFE

Dear God,

I hate my life. Everything seems troubling and meaningless. Endless demands on my time and energy overwhelm me. I feel as though I'm chasing the wind.[1]

Work drains my strength. The boss's disagreeable temperament creates tension in the office. Dysfunctional colleagues waste my time, and fear of a pink slip looms over my head. If I don't add income with overtime, bill collectors pound down the door. Worry drains every ounce of vitality.

Evenings fail to provide relief. Gavin expects dinner on the table by 6:30 p.m. sharp. Horrific news reports bombard our twenty-minute meal with video clips of crimes—kidnappings of children from school, road-rage, and mysterious viruses. Potential war threatens our daily lives.

After we eat, the teenagers in our unblended family argue over the car, refuse to comply with rules, and challenge every decision. Then *our* two little ones avoid their homework, beg to shop for Halloween costumes, and whine about bedtime. Where is Gavin's helping-hand amidst the chaos?

All the demands of suburban life on Hysteria Lane have taken their toll on my heart and soul. Internal and external expectations of perfection assault my well-being from every direction.

God, I'm so tired.

Rebecca

---

[1] Ecclesiastes 2:17

My Dear Rebecca,

My heart breaks for you, because your treadmill lifestyle robs you of joy and peace. You have grown weary and carry heavy burdens. You are so busy you don't have time to eat. You were created for relationship with Me above all else, but worldly demands and senseless chaos eroded our sacred time together. No wonder you're tired.

Creation itself speaks to your need for relaxation. I worked for six days, and on the seventh day, I rested. I blessed the seventh day and declared it holy[2] for *your* benefit.[3] You, too, have six days each week for your work. The seventh day provides you with opportunity to refresh your spirit and remember that I am your Holy God.[4]

Would you rather continue to struggle through each day defeated and depleted without Me?[5] Or are you ready to rely on Me and experience a purposeful, meaningful and peaceful life? Rebecca, only you can make that choice.

Come to Me and I will give you *permission* to rest. Seek Me with all your heart and live according to My word.[6] As you trust Me, you will find new strength to soar high on wings like eagles. You will run and not grow weary. You will walk and not faint.[7] I'll help you sort your priorities to use your time wisely, for not everything allowed is beneficial.[8]

Let's go off by ourselves now and find a quiet, special place to rest.[9] Collapse into My loving arms. Place your trust in Me, and I

[2] Genesis 2:2-3
[3] Exodus 16:29a
[4] Isaiah 58:13
[5] Isaiah 57:20
[6] Matthew 6:33
[7] Isaiah 40:31
[8] 1 Corinthians 10:23
[9] Hebrews 4:9

promise to give you hope for each new day.[10] Allow My pillar of strength to support you. Be still, and know that I am God.[11]

Let Me teach you how to live, for My ways make life easier to manage. For what do you benefit if you gain the whole world but lose your soul? Is anything in this world worth more than your soul?[12]

I love you, Rebecca.

God

God's Promise: Matthew 11:28-29

> Come to me, all of you who are weary and carry heavy burdens, and I will give you rest. Take my yoke upon you. Let me teach you, because I am humble and gentle at heart, and you will find rest for your soul.

---

[10] Psalm 62:5
[11] Psalm 46:10
[12] Matthew 16:26

Divine Exchange

Dear God

Dear Daughter

NO VALENTINE

Dear God,

With Valentine's Day around the corner, I'm supposed to be happy. Instead, disenchantment floods my mind, because I don't have a man to love me.

Heart-shaped balloons assault me at the grocery store. Pink and red candies of every sort clutter the mall. Even Seven-Eleven stocks roses for last-minute lovers. All I have is an ache in my heart.

The office provides no solace. Excited women gather to chat and giggle about upcoming dates, romantic dinners and jewelry they hope to receive. Cards and flowers adorn every desk—except mine. When I arrive home from work, no one greets me. Only darkness awaits.

Who cares that I'm late? Who knows if I'm sick or sad? Who shares my joys and sorrows?

It's not that I don't want someone to love. You know I've tried to develop meaningful relationships. But in the end, nothing lasts except disappointment. God, my loneliness drones louder than the annoying buzz of the refrigerator keeping me company at night.

Samantha

My Dear Samantha,

I've seen your heart trampled and betrayed as you wonder if you will ever find a suitable husband. I know how depressed you feel living alone—especially on a Hallmark holiday such as Valentine's Day.[1]

When you arrive home from work downcast, although you don't see me, I am waiting.[2] On days when your heart feels sick, I offer you My healing balm.[3] In the night as your tears fall, I treasure each one.[4]

Many women settle for mass-produced cards with sentiments that fade. But I wrote you a treasure of love letters in the Bible to express my everlasting love for you.[5] Samantha, My mind overflows with thoughts of you all the time, rather than merely one day a year. Red balloons pop. Chocolates disappear. Pink flowers wilt.[6] But My faithful love remains with you for eternity.[7]

My precious daughter, I know you need someone that's true and strong. If you give me your undivided affection, I'll lavish you with My love until you believe that I am the One you're trying to find to fill the hole in your heart.

Samantha, will you join me for supper at My house on February 14 to share bread and wine?[8] Will you be My forever Valentine?

Love,
God

God's Promise: Jeremiah 31:3

I have loved you with everlasting love. With unfailing love I draw you to Myself.

---

[1] Ecclesiastes 2:1
[2] Matthew 5:4
[3] Matthew 9:35b
[4] Psalm 56:8
[5] Jeremiah 31:3
[6] Isaiah 40:8
[7] Psalm 136
[8] Mark 14:22-25

Divine Exchange

Dear God

_____

_____

_____

_____

_____

_____

Dear Daughter

_____

_____

_____

_____

_____

THE RED COCKTAIL

Dear God,

Tomorrow brings forth my last chemotherapy treatment—the eighth red cocktail. With my body tired and my spirit zapped, my future looms like a bleak cloud.

Chemo caused a makeover. There is no health in my body, and I'm completely crushed.[1] Burning sensations pierce every joint, and any small movement brings tears to my eyes. The bottoms of both feet feel numb. On my left foot, my big toenail fell off first, followed by two others. On my right foot, toenail disintegration began with the baby toe. The pain in my back remains intolerable.

I vomit, and then dry heaves wrench my aching body. Then the cycle repeats over and over. Cheesecake, which I love, tastes bland and dry like flour. Unlike the first set of drugs, not a moment of peace exists between treatments. If remission doesn't occur after this nightmare, I swear I will never receive chemo again. Period. No matter what.

Then I think of my granddaughter, Parker, due to be born March 12, and I cling by a thread to your promise that you never give me more than I can bear with your help.[2]

But God, I'm tired. Without quality of life, what's the point of living? When do I give up my fight?

Laurie

---

[1] Psalm 38:7-8
[2] 1 Corinthians 10:13

My Dear Laurie

I have watched over you every second as you endured drinking each wretched cocktail. This battle stole your peace, health and security. You feel battered.[3] During this trial, you displayed a heroic fight of faith,[4] and watching you delights Me. Whenever you were able, you pursued righteousness, godliness, and love. Your faith beamed a laser of light for doctors, nurses, and family in your midst bringing Me glory.

I know with all you suffered, you lost perspective. But don't lose heart, my precious daughter, for I have a purpose for your life[5] far greater than your health. It is not fate, nor chance, nor luck, nor coincidence that you breathe at this very moment. I decided when you would be born and how long you would live. All the days ordained for you were written in My book[6] before one of them came to be.[7] Your life and breath are in My hands.[8]

Even now as you grow too weary to fight for the healing of your body and struggle for strength to endure,[9] I extend compassion and mercy.[10] In My perfect timing, you will realize that there is nothing that has happened to you that I do not use for good, to save many lives.[11]

Precious Laurie, I tell you, do not lose heart.[12] Release your burdens to Me, and I will carry you as we finish the race here on earth together. At the appointed time of your physical death, heaven awaits. When you arrive, you will receive a new body, for

[3] Bush, Elaine Greydanus. *Three Generations Fight Cancer Together: Lessons Learned on the Journey*. Central Florida: EA Books Publishing, 2017, 19.
[4] 1 Timothy 6:11b, 12
[5] Rick Warren, *The Purpose Driven Life: What on Earth Am I Here For?* (MI: Zondervan, 2002), 17, 22, 23
[6] Psalm 139:16
[7] Psalm 139:16
[8] Job 12:10
[9] Job 6:11
[10] James 5:11
[11] Genesis 50:19-20
[12] 2 Corinthians 4:16

your earthly body bears evidence of pain and suffering—the marks of Jesus.[13] Your true citizenship lies here with Me forever.[14]

Love,
God

God's Promise: James 1:12

God blesses those who patiently endure testing. Afterward, they will receive the crown of life that God has promised to those who love him.

---

[13] Galatians 6:17
[14] Philippians 3:20

Divine Exchange

Dear God

_____

_____

_____

_____

_____

Dear Daughter

_____

_____

_____

_____

_____

PRAGMATIC BREAKUP

Dear God,

Today Matthew *abruptly* ended our relationship.

Last week he declared his love for me, and today he says, *let's just be friends*. He didn't bother to call or arrange a meeting so I could look him in the eye and understand. This email arrived out of the blue.

> *Dear Angel, things in our relationship have changed. After a year of dating, I'm forced to come to grips with our ongoing differences. I've come to see the painful reality that, after all is said and done, we truly are in different places in life, and, therefore, not where we need to be to move forward in our relationship.*

> *There is no denying that we have experienced vastly different lifestyles. You have been accustomed to the finer things in life, and I can't conceive of that. I could never provide that standard of living for you or share that with you. We were raised in different cultures. Your manners feel right to you, and mine feel right to me. Despite having a low-level white-collar job, I am blue collar at heart. My comfort zone seems unacceptable to you.*

> *Our long-distance relationship means we are not able to share everyday life experiences which adds pressure to our relationship the few times we are able to be together. I'm more and more dissatisfied with "cyber-everything."*

> *Our different work schedules impact our relationship. When I'm off work, it's wonderful not having other demands on my time and energy and great to be able to*

give you whatever you need or desire. In reality, that freedom lasts only a few weeks a year. I don't have time to invest in our relationship.

Spiritually, we profoundly differ on what we think the Christian's everyday life experience should be like. Because God is sovereign, I thought we would be able to bridge the gap, but I don't feel comfortable with your preferences. What I regard as essential, and what you regard as essential don't align. The big difference in our spiritual worldviews appears too difficult to overcome.

Angel, all of these factors add pressure to our dating relationship so that it has become too burdensome to be healthy. What hasn't changed is that I would still like to be friends.

Fondly,
Matthew

God, I'm dumbstruck. We discussed none of this list. What about love? He didn't mention anything about our intimate love in his list of complaints against me. How do I face tomorrow without Matthew? I'm desperate without him.

Angel

My Dear Angel,

Today turned into a day of trouble for you, and you saw none of this coming. I am so sorry. The letter you spread before Me now broke your heart, and I hear your crying out for some way to cope with the disappointment and hurtful words slung in your face. You saw Matthew as a loyal man who valued your kind spirit and treasured your gentle loving heart. He complimented your eyes, enjoyed your femininity and seemed to protect your vulnerabilities.

He inched his way into your trust little by little, reassuring you all the while of his unconditional love for you. He continually sought deeper commitment from you as you dated, and in your mind's eye, you saw Matthew as your husband and friend for life.

Matthew's duplicity jarred your emotions, triggered your insecurities, and exposed your tender vulnerabilities. His insensitive manner in handling the end of your relationship harms your ability to trust men again. Being abandoned left you feeling ragged and torn, and hope deferred sickened your heart.[1] My dear Angel, he enticed you—no wonder you feel betrayed.

Along the way, you also caused each other to stumble and lost your footing by desiring each other above your relationship with Me. Together, your time in scripture and prayer decreased, and you neglected My word. Now you experience difficult consequences like silver in a crucible of suffering.[2] Angel, the time has come for you to let go and surrender Matthew to Me.

Although you can't change Matthew or his decision, the hours you once shared with him may now be spent basking in My tender loving care for you. Your emotional needs never burden Me as they did Matthew. I will pour my healing balm of grace into those wounded places. In your bleak moments, I will meet you in our quiet place and bless you with love, compassion and spiritual intimacy. I will wipe your tears and nurture the deepest groaning of your soul. I will pursue you with constant provision and faithful protection. I will anoint you with My pure love that never ends. With Me at your side, your time of darkness and despair will not go on forever.[3]

As you recover from the shock of rejection from the man you love, I remain your faithful companion. I know sadness permeates your soul, but as you grieve, I soothe your feelings of worthlessness. Your despair will diminish in my tender loving care. I never betray your trust—your heart remains safe with Me.

---

[1] Proverbs 13:12a
[2] Isaiah 48:10
[3] Psalm 30:5b

How precious are My endless thoughts about you, my special earth Angel—they cannot be numbered.[4]

You are exactly where I want you, because I know what's next for your life. Without the yoke between you and Matthew, you are now free to join Me on a fulfilling journey you could never have imagined in your wildest dreams. You have gifts and talents to be used for My wonderful purpose. The plans I have for you I decided long ago, and I'm ready to make them happen.

Many seeds of love planted into your heart are ready to sprout, and they will grow and flourish.[5] Along your spiritual journey, as you help others, they will see My love reflected in your eyes so beautiful to behold. Wherever you go, My heavenly angels will protect you.

Love,
God

God's Promise: Jeremiah 29:11

I know the plans I have for you—plans for good and not for disaster, to give you a future and hope.

---

[4] Psalm 139:3-17
[5] Isaiah 37:26, 31

Divine Exchange

Dear God

Dear Daughter

SHALLOW VAL

Dear God,

I feel unhappy all the time, but I don't know why.

My husband and I have everything—a Lexus SUV, a classic corvette, and a Mercedes in our four-car garage. Money in the bank. An amazing stock portfolio and investments in real estate. A trust fund. My closet, the size of Oprah's, overflows with designer clothes, cashmere sweaters, jewelry and shoes!

Shane, respected in the community as a leader, owns his law practice. He's handsome, wonderful, and fun. My career, which I love, also reaps success. Everyone on Hysteria Lane envies my *white-picket-fence* life.

Yet, when I look myself in the eye and tell myself the truth, I am never satisfied. Indeed, I do have everything—including discontentment, emptiness, and lack of peace.

God, what can I do to fill the hollow place in my heart?

Valerie

My Dear Val,

I am proud of all of your accomplishments. You have used your time to achieve far beyond what most people ever imagine. You have been blessed with many tangible rewards, including money, property, and possessions. Your many talents, invested strategically in your career, resulted in success and admiration. All of the energy you directed toward outstanding achievements paid big dividends.

Or did it?

Just as I am a Triune God[1] by nature, I created you, Val, with three aspects of your personality—physical, emotional, and spiritual.[2] You have mastered the development of the physical aspect of your character at the expense of the emotional and spiritual dimensions.

As you begin to strengthen your character in each area of your life, you will move toward finding greater fulfillment.

Consider for a moment how you relate to others. With your employees, are you approachable and willing to admit your mistakes, or do you take advantage of them for personal gain? What happens with your personal friendships? Are they acquaintances or genuine friends who know your weaknesses as well as your strengths?

Val, in your marriage, I know you admire Shane's career, and you feel lucky to have married him, because he comes from a wealthy family. But, have you checked your attitude lately? Do you take time to examine the causes of your negative emotions, or do you blame Shane for your disagreements without considering your part in creating problems? Do you hide your issues in order to maintain your image and status?

Precious, meaningful relationships require consideration of other's needs beyond your own gratification.[3] Bonding requires trust, which grows as you give of yourself to others. When you develop intimacy in relationships by giving, your life becomes more meaningful and satisfying.[4]

Yet, no matter how meaningful other people become in your life, it is not possible for them to always meet your needs and

---

[1] Matthew 28:19

[2] The Life Application Bible, NIV, Large Print (IL: Tyndale House Publishers, and Zondervan Publishing House, 1995), 10

[3] Ibid. 1984, 2262

[4] Proverbs 11:25

expectations. That is My design so you come to realize that you need a perfect relationship—with Me. I am the only one who can meet the deepest longings within your heart.[5]

When I look at your spirit, Val, I see a parched land.[6] When was the last time you walked with Me and talked with Me? Where do I fit in your tier of priorities? Do you believe that My words in Scripture apply to your everyday life?[7]

When you lay aside materialism and strive first to know Me, you will find Me.[8] I am waiting for you. The desires of your heart belong with Me, for I am He that cares for you. I will lead you to living beyond acquisitions. When you place Me at the center of your life and balance your emotional and physical needs, your life will be transformed. Then, you will find joy and peace.

Will you invite Me into your heart and begin a new journey of faith? I will take your hand, and meet you right where you are. Day by day, I will lead you to make your path straight.[9] I will help you rearrange your priorities, so each day will not be frazzled or fragmented. As you learn to delegate some responsibility to others, we will have more time together, and others will benefit and grow, too.

When you are ready to walk a spiritual journey with Me, I will wrap My Word around every obstacle in your way. You will come to believe that I am faithful to keep My promises.[10] With Me at the center of your life, your spirit will soar on the wings of the wind.[11]

---

[5] Philippians 4:19
[6] Jeremiah 12:11
[7] Ibid. 1239
[8] Proverbs 8:17
[9] Proverbs 4:11
[10] Proverbs 33:4
[11] Psalm 18:10

The new life I promise for you is more amazing than all you have acquired on Hysteria Lane. From the depths of your soul, you will begin to experience peace.[12] With Me, you will always find satisfaction and contentment—your life will be fulfilled.

Val, I fill the God-shaped hollow in your heart.

Love,
God

God's Promise: John 14:27a

> I leave you with a gift—peace of mind and heart.
> So don't be troubled or afraid.

---

[12] John 14:27

Divine Exchange

Dear God

_____

_____

_____

_____

_____

Dear Daughter

_____

_____

_____

_____

_____

ROAD RAGE

Dear God,

The other night, as we drove to Target, misty rain created slick pavement. When a car whipped past us to beat a truck, Mark got furious. As he jerked the steering wheel to avoid an accident, the offensive driver gestured. Mark accelerated. My foul words spewed.

"What do you think you are doing? %)&%#@*Let him pass."

Mark ignored me.

A vision of our mangled car and bodies skidded before my eyes. By the time we got home, I had a complete meltdown. Mark slammed the door.

"*I* was driving. *I* was in control. The situation looked different from the driver's seat. Why were you screaming at me? Did that help? Next time, if you're so smart, *you* drive."

This scenario repeats whenever Mark drives. When we encounter a dangerous situation, he ignores my fears, proving his lack of concern for my safety. God, My life's at stake, and he won't change his behavior. What should I do?

Patty

My Dear Patty,

I understand why you feel unsafe and helpless—road rage scares everyone. When someone attacks with a vehicle as a weapon, you become a defenseless victim. You lose a sense of security, and fear takes the wheel.

Mark has been given authority as the head of your household, which includes protecting his family. As such, he is accountable to Me for his behavior. From my perspective, he had no intention of causing you harm—that's the last thing he would ever do. He loves you, Patty, and he cares for you to the best of his ability.

I have given Mark free will to make decisions including how to drive. It is not your role to change him, and he is not on this earth to meet all of your expectations. However, you are in a position to make different choices for yourself. I certainly don't expect you to be victimized when you feel unsafe.

So what are *your* choices?

When you go out to dinner tomorrow night, why not drive your own car and meet at the restaurant? You both would have time to reflect on the cause of this scenario. Then, over dinner, discuss this problem from a new perspective.

In the meantime, reflect on these questions: What is your part in this ongoing power struggle? Have you noticed that barking orders only breeds defensiveness? Is your mode of communication respectful, or do you need to downshift your tone? Would you be safer with Mark if he were not distracted by your expletives during an emergency situation?

Patty, road-rage gives you an opportunity to respect your husband. When you berate, your tongue becomes like a serpent with words of venom.[1] Out of the same mouth come praise and cursing. You praise Me and curse your beloved, who was made in My likeness. My precious child, this should not be.[2] A wise woman guards her mouth, and her tongue keeps her from calamity.[3] Her gentle response turns away wrath.[4]

With a different approach to express your fears, you will discover that Mark cares for you with all his heart. Explain how you feel, and he will become empathetic. As he listens to your

---

[1] Psalm 140:3
[2] James 3:9-10
[3] Proverbs 21:23 NIV
[4] Proverbs 15:1

heart, he will see how his choices hurt you. If you speak words of encouragement and edification, perhaps his visible concern for your safety will accelerate.

As you work together toward a solution, will you trust Me to keep you safe?[5]

Let me reassure you, I am in the driver's seat of your life. When you find yourself in a fearful situation, pray to Me. I will soothe your frayed nerves, because I am your refuge and strength, always ready to help in times of trouble.[6] When you call on Me, I will answer you in the midst of your fears and show you the wonder of My great love.

Patty, I care about your marriage, your safety, and all matters of your heart.

Love,
God

God's Promise: Psalm 121:8

The Lord keeps watch over you as you come and go both now and forever.

---

[5] Psalm 18:2
[6] Psalm 46:1

Divine Exchange

Dear God

_____

_____

_____

_____

_____

Dear Daughter

_____

_____

_____

_____

_____

SECRETS ON HYSTERIA LANE

Dear God I'm Desperate

CHARRED HEART

Dear God,

A secret from my past haunts me even after all these years.

When I was fifteen, I met the coolest guy at Walmart. Kirk, who was nineteen, caused my heart to pound. He invited me to wild and wonderful parties. I thought if I joined his in-crowd, I wouldn't feel lonely. One night, filled with mischief and beer, we left the fun early. Kirk held me close as we giggled through the darkness to his truck.

Kirk promised, "Brianna, I will love you forever."

That fateful night, I lost my virginity. I thought I would feel special, but instead, I felt dirty. I didn't care because Kirk said he loved me. And to cover my guilt, I smoked. After months of our wild lifestyle, the *test* results revealed the truth—positive.

When I told Kirk, he lied, "Woman, that baby is not mine." He walked out.

Scared and alone, I cried, until my changing body exposed my secret. At least, I reasoned, the baby will love me.

Mother hounded me. "Brianna, how could you be so stupid to get pregnant? You have to get an abortion. I'll give you money and we'll lie to your father. No one will ever know. This mess doesn't have to ruin your life."

So the next day, we went to a clinic where the doctor "got rid of it." My baby was gone forever. No one ever found out my secret, but guilt still haunts my conscience day and night. The nightmare remains etched upon my charred heart. Since that fateful day, I've been ashamed and afraid to tell my unsuspecting husband. God, I was wrong. I need help.

Brianna

My Dear Brianna,

My child, I know how terrified you have been to share your secret with Me. But I've been waiting for you.[1] Don't you know, Brianna, My unending compassion overflows for you even in the midst of your difficulty.[2] You are not alone.

You dreaded going to the clinic that day. Your heart pounded. Trembling overwhelmed your body. Terror over the death of your unborn child assaulted you. Although you had no idea of My presence, I cared for you then,[3] and I love you still, Brianna.[4]

As you have discovered, an abortion results in difficult consequences. Your life will never be the same. Yet, the past can't rob you of My tender affection. No matter how many mistakes you make—past, present or future—nothing causes Me to stop loving you.[5]

I am pleased that you shared your secret with Me, even though you believed I would shun you. Filled with remorse, you fell to your knees, confessed your sin, and asked forgiveness.

My next step for you seems difficult, but if you choose to do what I say, you will reap rewards. It's time for you to trust John with your secret. When you both choose to admit your sins, forgive each other, and pray for each other, you will be healed. Your prayers will produce wonderful results in your relationship with Me and with him.[6]

---

[1] Isaiah 30:18
[2] Psalm 103:13
[3] Psalm 55:4-6
[4] 1 John 4:16
[5] Romans 8:38-39

Come now, Brianna. Let us settle this matter once and for all. You have surrendered your guilt and shame.[7] In exchange, I promise to sweep away your sin, scatter your offense like the morning mist, and surround you with My shield of grace.[8] I promise to shower you with My blessings,[9] replace your loneliness with joy and lead you to a place of peace.[10]

Brianna, you have had a long season to cry and grieve. You repented, and I have cleared your record and blotted out the stain of your sin forever.[11] A blanket of pure, white snow now covers your scarlet secret.[12] Now, I bless you with a season to laugh and a time to dance.[13]

Love,
God

God's Promise: Psalm 34:5

Those who look to the Lord for help will be radiant with joy; no shadow of shame will darken their faces.

---

[6] James 5:16
[7] 1 John 1:9
[8] Psalm 5:12
[9] Proverbs 10:6a
[10] Romans 15:13
[11] Psalm 32:1-2; 51:1-2
[12] Isaiah 1:18
[13] Ecclesiastes 3:4

Divine Exchange

Dear God

_____
_____
_____
_____
_____
_____

Dear Daughter

_____
_____
_____
_____
_____
_____

CHEATER

Dear God,

Month after month, I've cheated on my husband, because he never pays attention to me. Justin works seven days a week and refuses to help with the kids. When we first married, we talked and laughed for hours. Now he prefers to watch the sports channel or play video games.

With Justin busy and the kids in school, I feel lonely.[1] Searching online dating sites, I met Brian. Then Todd. And all the others.

God, I'm ashamed to tell you how I've sinned with these men. I want to stop myself, but I can't.[2] The harder I try, the more obsessed I become with targeting my next man. I know you disapprove, and I deserve your worst punishment.[3]

After each fling, I sneak home to shower and gulp down a martini. Or three. By the time Justin comes to bed, I've passed out. Thankfully, I don't have to look into his eyes. It's bad enough to look in the mirror at my own pitiful reflection.

Secret upon secret causes me to watch over my shoulder afraid someone will catch me. Lie after lie keeps my stomach tied in knots. Day after day, my frazzled nerves unravel.

---

[1] Psalm 102:6-8
[2] Romans 7:15
[3] Ezekiel 7:26-27

God, I'm desperate. I needed to feel loved, but instead I created this tangled-up mess I call my life. If you will help me, this time I'll do whatever you say. I promise.

Tiffany

My Dear Tiffany,

I've watched you knowing your choices would lead to anguish and despair. Difficult consequences always follow sin.[4] All the while, no matter how much you betrayed yourself and Justin, *I loved you dearly*.

Over and over you said, "I hate the things I do, but I can't help it.[5]" You blamed others refusing to take responsibility for your actions. Yet, no matter how often you failed, Tiffany, I still loved you.

As a result of your behaviors, you and Justin live together in silence. Deceit defines your marriage. Alcohol robs your joy. Fear and torment lurk to expose your secrets. Watching now as you hit rock bottom breaks My heart, but I love you with everlasting love, and now I want to draw you near to My heart.[6]

Facing the dark reality you created will cause gut wrenching remorse. Tiffany, because you have confessed your sexual sins and I am faithful, I forgive you.[7] As you persevere through this difficult time, I will care for you and lead you step by step from despair to hope.[8] I promise to remain by your side.[9] When you need comfort,[10] I will enfold you with love.

---

[4] Romans 6:23
[5] Romans 7:18
[6] Jeremiah 31:3
[7] Jeremiah 33:8
[8] Psalm 25:4
[9] Isaiah 49:13, 15
[10] Matthew 5:4

When you feel isolated, call My name. Walk with Me.[11] As we work through your pain together, pride will lose its grip on your heart. As you become faithful to Me, you will become faithful to Justin. Then I will crown you with beauty and replace your mourning with blessing.[12]

Tiffany, I will love you always and forever.

Love,
God

God's Promise: 2 Corinthians 5:17

> Anyone who belongs to Christ has become a new person. The old life is gone; a new life has begun!

---

[11] Psalm 23
[12] Isaiah 61:3

Divine Exchange

Dear God

_____

_____

_____

_____

_____

Dear Daughter

_____

_____

_____

_____

_____

iMATE

Dear God,

What I suspected has been revealed. A heavy load of lies, long hidden beneath the surface, exploded in my face today like a landmine. Instead of shrapnel, pain invades every part of my body, and resentment burns my soul. Brandon's a liar.

His heart spews destruction; his every word speaks deceit.[1] With his secret life of addiction to pornography exposed, I feel ambushed and degraded by his filth.

I researched facts about his behaviors, and I am shocked at what I learned. Sexual addiction is constructed with three building blocks—pornography, sexual fantasy, and masturbation.[2]

How can he love me while he lusts over images of other women? Am I so old and ugly that I no longer appeal to him? It's true my body lacks luster compared to those photographs, but his body has aged too. What did I do that drove him away? Why do I feel guilty when Brandon is the one who has ruined our marriage?

Like my heart, our family shattered at this disgusting revelation. Oh, God, I'm desperate. I want a divorce yesterday. What other choice do I have? How can I live another day sleeping with the enemy?

Emily

---

[1] Psalm 5:9

[2] Daniel Henderson, *Think Before You Look: Avoiding the Consequences of Secret Temptation* (TN: Living Ink Books, a division of AMG Publishers, 2005), 23.

My Dear Emily,

You have been bludgeoned by Brandon's sin against you—no wonder you feel violated. He broke his covenant marriage vows to you when he committed adultery in his heart.[3] The feeling that you do not measure up at the brunt of Brandon's disdain caused excruciating heartache. My dear daughter, you have been betrayed by the love of your life.[4]

I know the devastating pain you feel from discovering Brandon's obsession. He's blinded by addiction to believe that he can still cherish you, even though he is making pseudo-love to dozens of images of other women. When it comes to marriage, you deserve his exclusive love and romance.[5]

In your shock and confusion, *false* guilt plagues you. Brandon chose sin, which is not your fault. You are wonderfully made; nothing about you caused his fall into temptation. He made multiple unwise decisions on his path of deception filled with unhealthy and compulsive behaviors. The deeper pornography dug its claws into his lifestyle, the greater the negative consequences.[6] Unfortunately, your entire family now suffers.

Brandon has confessed to you the reality of his lifestyle, so you are set free from the *deception* that undermined your marriage. Consequently, he lost his integrity in your eyes, and a marriage void of trust lacks the necessary foundation for survival.[7] As you grieve, I will heal your despair. As for Brandon, he must now face the daunting reality of regaining your trust over time.[8]

Now that the prior form of your marriage has died, what do you do?

---

[3] Matthew 5:27-29
[4] Psalm 55:11-13
[5] Daniel Henderson, *Think Before You Look*, 143
[6] Ibid. 4
[7] Ibid. 134
[8] Beall, Cindy, *Healing a Marriage When Trust is Broken*, Harvest House Publishers, 2016

There is no quick fix, but I promise to help you untangle this hotbed of lies. What you need first is a time to grieve,[9] because tears unshed become stones in your heart, smother you in a blanket of sadness, and weigh down your spirit. As this difficult process of mourning begins, spend time alone with Me to see your true self—the one I love—not the one Brandon rejected.[10]

As you wade through these deep rivers of disappointment and sadness, don't lose heart, for I, the Lord your God remain with you. Nothing can consume you, because you are mine.[11] Minute by minute, My angels protect you and care for you along this unfamiliar pathway.[12]

I hear your raging thoughts. *What about Brandon? This mess is his fault.*

Although your marriage of the past can no longer be sustained, please don't give up on Brandon. After all, you've been married 21 years. Instead, even as your emotions rage defensively and you feel like you're hanging upside down by a thread, choose to forgive him as I have forgiven you. Your merciful act of obedience sets into motion my process of reconciliation and begins a series of molts to shed many layers of anger and bitterness that lead to the radical transformation you desire.

Brandon chose to face his addiction, repented of his sins and surrendered his life to Me. Now I'll help him turn away from the ever-present erotic images and battle the resulting chemical rushes that dominate his brain.[13] I am able to renew his mind with My truth,[14] and teach him to discipline his conduct by biblical principles rather than emotional impulses. He's ready and willing to delay immediate gratification for the goal of restoration.[15]

---

[9] Ecclesiastes 3:3
[10] Linda Rooks, *Broken Heart on Hold: Surviving Separation* (CO: Life Journey, an imprint of Cook Communications Ministries, 2006), 144
[11] Isaiah 43:2
[12] Matthew 26:53
[13] Daniel Henderson, Ibid
[14] Romans 12:2
[15] Ibid, 64

Reconciliation with Brandon will be both delicate and difficult. Humanly speaking, your marriage may seem to be over, but remember that I AM God Almighty. With Me, everything is possible.[16] For now, each of you must walk separate parallel paths as I tear down the strongholds of the past and heal your emotions with My amazing grace.

Cling to Me as you grow spiritually, trusting and obeying my wise counsel. With My help, your marriage will become a spring of living water. Yes! A great new pathway, named the Highway of Holiness,[17] will break through as I prepare your hearts for a Godly reunion. You will become like trees planted along a riverbank, with roots deep into the water.[18]

Take My hand now, sweet Emily. Surrender your marriage to Me. Walk with Me by faith without a glimpse of the many blessings that lie ahead. Draw closer to Me as the depths of your soul gradually heal—one day at a time. As your protector and shield, I stand by your side. Trust Me to be your solid rock.[19]

Love,
God

God's Promise: Peter 5:10b

> After you have suffered a little while, God, in His kindness, will restore, support, and strengthen you, and He will place you on a firm foundation.

---

[16] Matthew 19:26
[17] Isaiah 35:7a, 8a
[18] Jeremiah 17:8
[19] Ecclesiastes 3:1-8

Divine Exchange

Dear God

Dear Daughter

PAPER OR PLASTIC

Dear God,

You don't know me, but you may know my husband, Stanley. On television commercials, he mows our lawn riding his John Deere past our beautiful home, swimming pool and SUV. He's the funny looking guy with a big plastic smile on his face.

"I'm Stanley Johnson.

"I've got a great family.

"I've got a four-bedroom house in a great community.

"Do you like my car? It's new.

"I belong to the local golf club.

"How do I do it?

"I'm in debt up to my eyeballs.

"I can barely pay my finance charges.

"Somebody help me."[1]

The truth is, we *have* purchased everything he mentioned. Along with lots of toys he didn't mention. God, I'm worried about the accumulation of debt—up to our eyeballs. Stanley and I argue daily concerning money. How could this *happy family* possibly enjoy the good life in the suburbs on Hysteria Lane? We live a lie.

Somebody help me? God, will you help me?

Jessica

---

[1] www.LendingTree.com, TV Advertisement

My Dear Jessica,

Yes. Of course I know Stanley. I also know you. Indeed, I have numbered the hairs on your heads.[2] How pleasing for Me to help you navigate your way through your money-maze. When you call on Me, I love to teach you My ways and bless your life.

Your use of money reflects *and* affects the nature of your relationship with Me.[3] Your spending choices indicate your fundamental values, so let's compare your *beliefs* to Mine. Do you believe *I* own your resources, or do you believe that *you* own them?

Let me remind you, the whole earth I established upon the waters.[4] All of the resources you enjoy—material possessions, abilities, knowledge, skills and relationships—belong to Me.[5] You and Stanley have been chosen as executors of My Trust Fund entrusted with decisions regarding the dispensation of My resources. Your responsibilities include taking care of My creation[6] and building My Kingdom within your sphere of influence.

At first, management of my estate may seem like an overwhelming task, but I do not leave you without help. First, come to Me in prayer for guidance, and I will generously provide you with wisdom.[7] Then, feed the hungry. Offer hospitality and clothing to those in need. Care for orphans and widows in their distress.[8] Visit prisoners and tend to those who are sick.[9]

---

[2] Luke 12:7
[3] Larry Burkett, *Caretakers Of God's Blessings: Using Our Resources Wisely* (USA: Crown Financial Ministries, 2002), 7.
[4] Psalm 24:1-2
[5] Ibid.14
[6] Genesis 1:27-28; 2:15
[7] Proverbs 2:6
[8] James 1:27
[9] Matthew 25:34-40

Jessica, when you and Stanley serve others instead of feeding your own greed, I bless your life in full measure, pressed down, shaken together to make room for more, and running over. Whatever measure you use in giving, large or small, it will be used to measure what is given back to you.[10]

Will you continue to use credit cards and accumulate debt? Or are you ready to become My trustworthy stewards based on what I provide? You decide—paper or plastic?

Love,
God

God's Promise: Psalm 37:5

Commit everything you do to the Lord.
Trust Him and He will help you.

---

[10] Luke 6:38

Divine Exchange

Dear God

Dear Daughter

VICTORIA'S SECRET

Dear God,

Something happened last summer that smothered me in shame. I've never shared this experience with anyone, but this secret burns inside my heart.

One unsuspecting, delightful Saturday, I went to the beach alone. Gentle laps of waves soothed my frayed nerves. Seagulls circled and sandpipers scurried. Pelicans watched in anticipation as fishermen cast their lines. To my delight, children giggled and frolicked as they built sandcastles.

As the afternoon waned away, dark clouds crept in. Little by little, beachgoers packed picnic baskets, folded their umbrellas, and headed home, but I stayed and enjoyed the light sprinkle of rain.

When the showers intensified and everyone deserted the beach, the overhang of the raised boardwalk provided me with shelter. As a lone dolphin frolicked close to the shoreline, I sensed something amiss and glanced upward to the deck overhead. There stood a man with his face covered by a hoodie.

My heart stopped when he exposed himself.

Driving home, I felt ashamed, and questions tortured my mind. *What did I do to provoke this? Why would that man torment me in this perverted way? Why is this world so scary?*

Going to the beach risks my safety. Mothers fear for their children at school, because pedophiles lurk by playgrounds. The evening news reports robberies, rapes, and endless predators against innocent victims.

God, how do I stay safe in this crazy world?

Victoria

My Dear Victoria,

I remember that particular day you went to the beach. Knowing you were alone, I watched out for you. Your audible cry for help, brought Me to your rescue immediately.[1] I promise to protect you always, because you are My precious child.

> When you feel hopeless, and don't know what to do,
> *cry out* to Me.

> When emotional or physical pain pierces your body,
> *cry out* to Me.

> When bad news engulfs you, and anguish grips your soul,
> *cry out* to Me.[2]

I am your God Most High, the supreme ruler of the universe, filled with power, knowledge and wisdom. I provide protection as I hover over you. Everything you need, I am ready, willing, and able to accomplish. I will move heaven and earth for you. I want to act on your behalf, to meet your specific needs.[3]

> When you need mercy, *cry out* to Me.

> When you need forgiveness, *cry out* to Me.

> When sudden disaster overtakes you, *cry out* to Me.[4]

If someone approaches you with the intention to harm, like the situation you faced at the beach, you must deal with two forces— physical and spiritual. When you cry out *help me Jesus,* the evil forces must confront My powerful forces. Since no evil can defeat Me, your cry for help in times of distress could save your life.[5]

---

[1] Dr. Charles Stanley, When We Cry Out To God (GA: In Touch Ministries, Sermon on CD MM281), www.intouch.org.

[2] Ibid

[3] Ibid

[4] Ibid

[5] Ibid

I may not change your circumstances if they serve My higher purpose, but I never leave you to fend for yourself. Instead, I delight in answering your cry for help and always provide what you need to cope.[6]

I may change your spirit or your attitude by providing contentment, peace, or joy in the midst of your situation. I may guide you to a new action or equip you to handle what you face. Because I am omnipresent, I see you no matter what happens, and when you *cry out to Me*, I answer your cry.[7]

My precious Victoria, I respond immediately, because I love you.

Love,
God

God's Promise: Isaiah 65:24

I will answer you before you even call to me. While you are still talking about your needs, I will go ahead and answer your prayers.

---

[6] Proverbs 15:8b

[7] Dr. Charles Stanley, When We Cry Out To God (GA: In Touch Ministries, Sermon on CD MM281), www.intouch.org.

Divine Exchange

Dear God

Dear Daughter

ZACH'S FINAL LIE

Dear God,

My mutilated heart hurts. You saw our divorce proceedings today. The scene replays in my mind, over and over and over, gripping me with torment.

"Bailiff, are all parties present in order to proceed?" the judge asked.

"Your Honor, 'the husband' is present by prearranged teleconferencing, audio without video. 'The wife' is present. Her attorney is delayed without explanation."

In a split second, a glare from the judge met my bloodshot eyes. My cold hands trembled. The knot tightened in my nauseous stomach. *Where on earth is my attorney?*

"Thank you bailiff. You may proceed to swear in both parties."

With the tap of his gavel, The Honorable Harrison Jeffries Burke, III opened case number FL 911-321-007.

From the hidden speaker, I heard the voice of my husband, once tender with love, now hardened with contempt, "I solemnly swear to tell the truth, the whole truth, nothing but the truth, so help me God."

Oh God, what happened to us?

"Mr. Bolton, you have presented a petition before this Circuit Court for the final judgment to legally end your marriage of 23 years. Is that correct?"

End. Petition. Final judgment. God, how could this be happening? Can't I at least look him in the eye?

"Yes, Your Honor."

"Mr. Bolton, I understand from the documents presented by your attorney, Ms. Wells, that all material possessions, finances, joint assets have been divided. Both parties agreed with terms set by mediation. Is that correct?"

What about hopes and dreams divided? Hearts divided.

"Yes."

"Have the required legal documents been signed and witnessed?"

"Yes."

"Do you understand, Mr. Bolton, that this court regards the divorce of your wife of 23 years to be serious in nature? You made a vow of marriage ratified by this State. The court does not take those vows lightly."

The COURT doesn't take vows lightly. How can YOU take them lightly?

"Yes."

"Do you understand that my decision regarding your marriage today is final and irrevocable?"

Final? Irrevocable? I swallowed the lump in my throat.

"Yes, Sir."

"Mr. Bolton, before you make this serious decision final, the court would like to offer an opportunity for you and your wife to receive counseling in order to reconcile? This would delay your divorce for a designated period of time by court order for the purpose of reconciliation. Would you like for the court to proceed in that direction?"

"No. I tried everything. Nothing helped," he lied.

Judge, he just lied in court! He hasn't tried. God, he lied. Did you hear that?

As I burst into tears, Judge Burke again looked toward me, this time with compassion.

"I understand from your testimony, Mr. Bolton, that you request this court to terminate your marriage. Is that correct?"

"Yes. Absolutely. The sooner the better. I'm done."

"Mr. Bolton, what additional comments would you like to make for the record?"

"Judge, listen. She caused these problems. I tried everything. Nothing worked. So I'm done. That's it."

My hand automatically formed the sign of the cross as if to protect my heart.

"Mrs. Bolton, your husband has petitioned this court to end your marriage. He has stated *under oath* that your marriage is irrevocably broken. You have heard his testimony—beyond reconciliation. Since your attorney is not present, do you have anything you would like to add for the record?"

Dumbstruck, I fumbled for words. Weeping robbed me of clarity. With tissues shredded, I used my hand to wipe my nose. Before I could collect my thoughts to respond, Ms. Wells objected.

"Your Honor, Mr. Bolton has made his petition to the court to end this marriage. He has testified under oath that their differences are irreconcilable. Mediation finalized the division of assets. No minor children are involved in this case. Under section 10, paragraph 6b of code, Mr. Bolton has the legal right for this petition for divorce to be granted. I request, Your Honor, that the court proceed with signing the final documents without further ado."

"Mrs. Bolton, do you have anything you would like to add for the record?" the judge repeated.

Shamed to silence I said, "No Sir."

I can't breathe. How could I add anything for the record?

"By the power vested in me, the dissolution of this marriage is final. Ms. Wells, will you please present the appropriate papers to the bailiff for legal documentation and signatures. Bailiff, will you please bring forth the next case."

Papers shuffled. Chairs and people moved. In a heap of defeat, I collapsed face down on the table and sobbed.

With the touch of a stranger's gavel, my destiny changed forever. Oh dear God, I'm scared. Divorce. Why, God? Why? I prayed. I tried. I prayed. What will I do? How will I survive?

Julie

My Dear Julie,

I'm here for you. I know how this divorce harmed your heart.[8] Your husband's betrayal tangled your emotions and caused you to lose sight of My everlasting love for you. Don't be afraid My precious daughter. I will care for you.[9] Take My hand. You are safe with Me. I'll help you survive. With compassion and tenderness, I draw you to Myself.[10]

Julie, your husband and I see you quite differently. In My sight, you were a wife of noble character, virtuous and capable, more precious than rubies.[11] I treasure you—body, soul, and spirit. I always listen to your heart and never hurt your feelings. You are a woman who deserves to be cherished. Although your husband

---

[8] Genesis 50:20
[9] Genesis 50:21
[10] Jeremiah 31:3
[11] Proverbs 31:10

won the divorce case, I have come to comfort[12] your broken heart and grant you favor.[13]

For now you grieve. When your season of sorrow ends, I will give you a crown of beauty for ashes, a joyous blessing instead of mourning, and festive praise instead of despair. You will grow strong like a great oak that I have planted for My glory. I will revive your heart and rebuild your life. Instead of shame, dishonor, and embarrassment, you will enjoy a double share of honor, a double portion of prosperity, and everlasting joy will be yours.[14]

Julie, because of My everlasting covenant, you will be faithfully rewarded for your unjust suffering. Instead of seeing you with pity, everyone will realize that I have blessed you and overwhelmed you with joy. You will become more beautiful than you were on your wedding day.[15]

Even if the mountains move and the hills disappear, My faithful love for you will remain. My covenant of blessing will never be broken.[16] Covered in My tender, bountiful love, you will not only survive, you will *thrive*.

No gavel breaks My promise to love you with everlasting love.

Love,
God

God's Promise: Isaiah 54:5

Your Creator will be your husband; the 'Lord of Heaven's Armies' is his name! He is your Redeemer, the Holy One of Israel, God of all the earth.

---

[12] Matthew 5:4
[13] Isaiah 61:2
[14] Isaiah 61:1, 4-6
[15] Isaiah 61:8-10
[16] Isaiah 54:10

Divine Exchange

Dear God

Dear Daughter

GONE WITH THE WIND

Dear God I'm Desperate

MRS. McDONALD'S TEST

Dear God,

All of my prenatal tests indicate that we are expecting a precious baby girl. Yet, my tears of joy mix with disappointment and fear.

Dr. Evans said, "Mrs. McDonald, I'm so sorry to have to tell you, the prenatal *chorionic villus sampling* for chromosomal abnormalities indicates your baby will be born with Down syndrome.[1] With your CVS positive, I'm required to inform you that you need to decide about an abortion by next Tuesday."

My thoughts swirled. My head throbbed. My heart raced. I felt my face flush as anger flooded my body. I wanted to yell at the top of my lungs, *Doctor Evans, what are you saying? What does state law have to do with my baby? How can they control a deadline for a life-changing decision like this? I can't even think.*

When Dr. Evans closed the door behind him, I sobbed. He left me alone in a stark room on a metal table, with nothing but a cold, hard question. *Do I get an abortion?*

Mother said yes, of course you need an abortion. "Emily, don't take a chance. If you have that baby, you will regret your decision for the rest of your life."

Why did I ask her?

John's parents blame my side of the family for the *problem* stating there is no genetic predisposition on their side of the family for Down syndrome.

[1] WEB MD © 2005 WebMD, Inc. www.webmd.com/baby/chorionic-villus-sampling

John feels angry and confused. "Honey, our parents could be right. After all, this is the first time they have ever agreed about anything."

Nobody wants to be embarrassed or shamed by an *imperfect* baby. Yet, my heart of hearts screams *NO*. I'm keeping her—I love Grace Alexis McDonald with all my soul. God, I'm desperate. What should I do?

Emily

My Dear Emily,

I know this news comes as a shock to you. There is no shame in your situation. Nothing is wrong with you. Nothing is wrong with John.

I am the Creator[2] of all life, and I formed a special daughter in your womb.[3] Who but Me decides if a baby is worthy to be born? Who but Me sets the standards of appearance and capabilities? I *chose* you as parents of this special child of Mine knowing your hearts overflow with love. You can provide the care and protection she needs.

Relatives may not understand. Some may pity you. Others may consider you crazy for not getting an abortion, but I bless those who do what is right in My eyes.[4]

John shares your fears and biggest question—will we be capable of loving this child? When he brings his worries and heartaches to Me, he will realize the blessing I have bestowed upon you. Together, I will help you face the opposition of well-meaning family and friends.

---

[2] Genesis 1:1
[3] Isaiah 44:2
[4] Matthew 5:10

Emily, have you and John ever met a child with Down syndrome? Let me encourage you with words from Pam, a proud mother of a DS child:

"If you're welcoming a new baby with DS into your family, you probably have many questions and concerns . . .

"Babies with the disorder are typically more like other developing infants than they are different. You'll find there's great diversity in terms of personality, learning styles, intelligence, appearance, compliance, humor, compassion, creativity, and congeniality.

"Children with DS look more like their families than they do one another. They have a full complement of emotions and attitudes and grow up to live independent lives with varying degrees of support.

"Down syndrome will not be the most interesting thing about your daughter. Remember that raising any child fills your life with unimaginable delight and difficulties. Your child with DS will benefit from the same care, attention, and inclusion in community life that helps every child grow.

"Individuals with DS may be identified by numerous physical attributes:

• Beautiful almond shaped eyes, striking Brushfield's on iris

• Single palmar crease on one or both hands

• Small features

• Exceptional social intelligence

• High rate of congenital heart defects

"Although children with DS are early customers for extensive health evaluations, keep in mind that every child deserves to be surrounded by people who love, respect, and admire all children.

"Thousands of young people with DS are quietly going on with their lives with dreams and the determination to reach their goals. They learn in regular classrooms in neighborhood schools with the children who will become their co-workers, neighbors, and adult friends. Young adults hold diverse and meaningful jobs, maintain their own households, and make significant contributions to their communities.

"Try to get some rest. You're allowed to feel however you feel, and so are others who love you and your baby. You deserve congratulations and wonderful gifts. Take time to welcome and enjoy your baby — she'll grow up fast."[5]

Emily, by keeping Gracie, as with every child, you will enjoy both blessings and troubles.[6] Although My ways are not always easy, don't be afraid, for I am with you. Don't be discouraged, for I am your God. I will strengthen you and help you. I will hold you up with My victorious right hand.[7] As you parent your new baby, you will experience peace in your heart.[8]

Love,
God

God's Promise: Psalm 119:1-2

Joyful are people of integrity who follow the instructions of the Lord. Joyful are those who obey His laws and search for Him with all their hearts.

---

[5] Pam Wilson, *Welcoming Babies with Down Syndrome*, www.babycenter.com.
[6] 2 Corinthians 4:16-18
[7] Isaiah 41:10
[8] John 14:27

Divine Exchange

Dear God

_____

_____

_____

_____

_____

Dear Daughter

_____

_____

_____

_____

_____

PECULIAR NEW NORMAL

Dear God,

After a grueling battle with breast cancer, remission provides relief. However, with the resulting physical limitations, constant aggravations plague me, and lymphadenitis in my left arm requires constriction and interrupts my sleep.

As I adjust to this peculiar new normal, one question still haunts me. Why do prisoners sitting in jail live long healthy lives while good people suffer?

For instance, my nephew Kyle's two beautiful daughters watched helplessly as their mother suffered through years of chemotherapy. When she went into remission, hope filled their hearts, but after only sixteen months, the cancer returned with a vengeance. Emma died three days before Christmas. Couldn't Emma have lived to celebrate Jesus' birthday with them one last time?

You plucked this special woman away from her family, while a healthy rapist sits in jail watching TV on taxpayer's money enjoying a long, healthy life. Why do you rob Kyle of the love of his life and leave him forlorn as a widower at only 34 years old?

God, why do You allow good people to suffer?

Lori

My Dear Lori,

I know your body has suffered excruciating pain, and I hear your heart cry out against the injustices you see in the world all around you. I understand why you question the endless suffering you observe. Why don't exploiters meet a speedy punishment? Life seems unfair.[1]

Through no fault of your own, you lost your health, but your pain brought you to brokenness. When suffering removed your protective shield, you no longer pretended that your life was perfect, and you felt powerless. As you were stripped of false securities, you *needed* Me. When you wrestled with the essence of your existence, you *depended upon* Me.

In response to your asperity, you could have wallowed in misery with an endless pity party, pointing your angry finger as you questioned My justice. You could have become arrogant, denounced My existence, and pretended you no longer cared about Me.

Instead, in your distress, you responded with maturity and allowed Me to touch your heart and save your crushed spirit.[2] With an amazing display of faith, you thanked Me for your blessings and shouted praises with your raspy voice. Your pain and suffering led you to a deeper reliance upon Me.

The prisoner you view as appeased in life remains confined behind bars, constricted by metal shackles. Everywhere he goes he drags a ball and chain of shame and guilt. His mind replays details of every bloody crime he committed like the constant rerun of a horror film.

He wastes away in a pool of his own misery. He sleeps on a hard, dirty mattress haunted by never-ending nightmares. Perverse seduction by his fellow inmates becomes a welcome distraction. Confined to a cell and chained to his own personal hell, not even

---

[1] *The Life Recovery Bible* (IL: Tyndale House Publishers, Inc., 1998), 635
[2] Psalm 51:17

the blessing of an illness distracts him from torment. Alone he faces the ugly man in the mirror tortured day and night by the constant drip of his conscience. Rejected by society and trapped in his mental dungeon of darkness and death, he lives shamed and disgraced—without hope.

Will his brokenness lead him to Me?

Lori, while you suffer from disease in your body, the prisoner suffers from disease of his soul. The desire of My heart is that everyone turn to Me for salvation. I shelter people oppressed by their circumstances when they turn their hearts to Me. I become a refuge in times of trouble for those who search for Me and trust in Me. I avenge murder cases for the helpless and never ignore the cries of those who suffer. I am known for my justice.[3]

The constructive path you chose during your season of suffering allowed time for our many heart-to-heart talks.[4] Even in the midst of your intolerable physical pain, you drew near to My heart. I have allowed you and the prisoner to suffer much hardship. To both of you, I am just, slow to anger, abounding in love and faithfulness.[5] I pardon sins and forgive transgressions.[6]

Lori, you asked the proverbial question of all time, "Why do people suffer?" You desire to comprehend My incomprehensible ways.[7] The answers exist beyond your grasp this side of Heaven, because My ways remain higher than your ways.[8] Circumstances you see are like the tip of an iceberg; the underside that I orchestrate stretches into the depths of each human soul with details invisible to you. That's why I give you the vital gift of faith—you need to depend on Me to navigate the waters of your life, especially when you don't understand.

---

[3] Psalm 9:7-8
[4] *The Life Recovery Bible*, Step 2, Persistent Seeking, 651
[5] Psalm 86:15
[6] Micah 7:18
[7] Job 38:18
[8] Isaiah 55:9

Faith trusts without understanding.

Faith provides confidence that My promises will happen.

Faith assures you about what you cannot see.[9]

I promise, all that occurs I use for My good purposes for those who trust in Me,[10] and in the end, every person receives My perfect justice.[11] By faith, trust that I am sufficient, all you need to deal with the ambiguities of life.

When you seek Me first above all else, [12] both your heart and mind find satisfaction. I teach you to live by faith without fear, trusting in My sovereign, tender care. In My loving arms, you will find peace, because everything that touches your life filters through My benevolent hands.

Lori, this world is not what it was meant to be with all this pain, all this suffering. But there's a better place waiting for you— Heaven. Every tear will be wiped away; every sorrow and sin erased. Where the streets are golden, and every chain is broken. Fear will be gone, and you will be in My open arms where you belong.

In Heaven, where you will be free at last, we'll dance forever on seas of amazing grace.[13]

Love,
God

God's Promise: Romans 8:18

You can be sure that what people suffer now is nothing compared to the Glory I will reveal later.

---

[9] Hebrews 11:1
[10] Romans 8:28
[11] Job 36:17b
[12] Matthew 6:33
[13] Chris Tomlin, *Home*, https://www.youtube.com/watch?v=twL3v5r8s6o

Divine Exchange

Dear God

Dear Daughter

LEAVING ON A JET PLANE

Dear God,

As the dreaded day approaches, mixed emotions trouble my mind. My baby, beloved Meghan, is leaving for college. The prestigious university of her dreams seems as far away from home as another planet. Was I crazy to support that decision? Yet, Megan danced with joy to be accepted, and she's ready.

But am I?

All year we have joked and cried over the "lasts." Last football game. Last prom. Last peeks through the Venetian blinds at teenage boys filled with high hopes as they ring the doorbell. Soon I must face reality—life without Meghan.

Sending Meghan to kindergarten hurt, but college seems worse. I feel useless and lonelier than lonely. In two weeks, my only child leaves by jet plane, and I don't know when she'll be back again.

Horror stories and alarming news reports on television portray dangers on campuses. Fraternity parties roar out of control. Coed dorms with no rules cause concern. What if she abuses drugs? What if she gets raped walking across campus at night? What if she gets shot?

God, I'm frantic with worry. Will you help me?

Michelle

My Dear Michelle,

I know you feel lonely and sad at the thought of an empty nest. Already your emotions rise and fall like a roller coaster, because your daily schedule will no longer include Meghan. I also know the intensity of love between you and Meghan. With separation, you face a bittersweet transition—joy mixed with heartache. Your role as Meghan's mother changes, and you fear for her future without your constant protection.

Alarming news reports, a sad reality of the times, trigger anxiety and rob you of peace. But what can you change by worrying about tomorrow?[1] My precious daughter, you prepared Meghan for the next phase of her life with practical safeguards in the event she faces danger. Also, you provided a solid spiritual foundation[2] upon which to build her life. You trained her in the way she should go.[3]

Do you remember when you went to college? Although you left your home and family, I didn't leave you.[4] I remained faithful to you, and I will remain faithful to Meghan.[5] And just as you endured troubles[6] during college, Meghan, too, will face difficulties. Since much of her struggle will be against spiritual forces, I will provide her with My protective armor.[7]

My belt of truth will guard against believing the lie that bad choices are good. My breastplate of righteousness protects Meghan's heart—the seat of her emotions and self-worth—the wellspring of life.[8] My shield of faith deflects insults, setbacks and temptations. My helmet of salvation dispels doubt that I am her God and I love her. Walking with My footgear, others will see that I am the source of her confidence and peace in the midst of college

---

[1] Matthew 6:34
[2] Matthew 7:24
[3] Proverbs 22:6a
[4] 1 Chronicles 28:20
[5] Psalm 100:5
[6] Psalm 34:19
[7] Ephesians 6:12-17
[8] Proverbs 4:23

stress. My sword, the Word of God, and My Spirit will guide her through the most difficult maze of decisions.

Although your responsibilities to Meghan now shift, she remains your beloved daughter and a treasured young woman.[9] First and foremost, during this life-changing transition, she needs your prayers.[10] As you both adjust to your new roles as mother and daughter, you will discover new and special ways to relate to one another.

Michelle, will you entrust Meghan to Me? Will you place your beloved baby in My outstretched arms and commit her to My tender care? [11]

And now, My precious daughter, what about your life, your hopes and dreams placed on the back burner long ago? As you and I journey together in this new season, will you trust Me with your hearts?

Love,
God

God's Promise: Philippians 4:6-7

> Do not be anxious about anything, but in every situation, by prayer and petition, with thanksgiving, present your requests to God. Then the peace of God, which transcends all understanding, will guard your hearts and your minds in Christ Jesus.

---

[9] Psalm 144:12b
[10] Matthew 21:21-23
[11] Psalm 91:4

Divine Exchange

Dear God

_____

_____

_____

_____

_____

_____

Dear Daughter

_____

_____

_____

_____

_____

_____

THE COLOR PURPLE

Dear God,

Scott died. Although my brother and I parted ways years ago because of rifts from the past, his beloved wife asked me to tend to his eight-year-old daughter, Sophie, at his funeral. I have no children, and I barely know my niece. Why would she be allowed to go to the service in the first place? Isn't she too young?

I don't even want to go to his memorial much less help out.

God, I'm at a loss. What should I do?

Amanda

My Dear Amanda,

Although you feel uncomfortable with this situation, and you wrestle with your own grief, you will not regret helping your sweet niece at such a time as this. Since it is difficult to understand the needs of a child who has lost her father, I share this story written by a woman who lost her dad as a child.

I remember my first funeral—I was eight years old when daddy died. Although I was too young to comprehend the full impact of this experience, I knew a cloud hung over our family like early morning fog.

That bitter-cold December day in Arlington National Cemetery, Aunt Ellen, who I had met only once, led me to a small chapel. As she squeezed my hand, the shell I had hidden in my white glove, poked through–my favorite purple shell that Daddy had given me.

Once inside she said, "Sit still and be quiet."

She scared me, so I did as I was told.

Soon I heard nice music, and Aunt Ellen whispered in my ear, "Here comes your daddy." Excited, I looked in the direction she pointed, but then I felt confused, because I didn't see him. What I saw instead was a big fancy box with a flag on top carried by men in uniforms like daddy wore to work. I glanced at Aunt Ellen, but I knew by her face this was no time for questions.

After church we walked down a grassy hill toward a carnival tent.

Aunt Ellen repeated, "Sit still and be quiet."

I tried to obey, but this time I wiggled. I had on my fancy Sunday dress with my black patent leather shoes, and chill bumps covered my bare legs as they touched a frozen metal chair.

Next, Aunt Ellen warned, "Cover your ears, and count to twenty-one. Don't be afraid."

I had no idea what would happen next. But, again I did what I was told, because everyone was strange and quiet gathered around that church box. Then I heard gunshots that scared me to death.

When the grownups finished talking, we walked up the hill and got into a black, strange car instead of our tan station wagon. I saw Reverend Harrison helping Mother up the hill, because something was definitely wrong.

The next day I went back to school. All the kids pointed at me and whispered to each other. They stayed away from me like I had cooties. Daddy never came home from work that day. Mother never mentioned daddy again, so neither did I. It seemed as if he just disappeared—except for the Purple Heart from his bureau.

Amanda, my precious daughter, I have a soft spot in My heart for children. What you do for your niece, you do for Me.[1] I will sustain you through your grief with My love and compassion. To

---

[1] Matthew 25:40

you I will disclose Sophie's needs, so you may help her through this huge hurdle in her life.

In addition, through this loss, I will expose your own emotional detachment, break down your walls of aloofness, and overpower your fears. I'll teach you how to build deep relationships and become the kind of person I want you to be.[2]

May you have ears to hear[3] and eyes to see[4] all the secrets I reveal to you.

Love
God

God's Promise: Mark 10:16

> Jesus takes the children in his arms, places his hands on them, and blesses them.

---

[2] Gail Porter. *Life Through Loss*, EABooks, Inc., 2014, 3
[3] Matthew 13:9
[4] Luke 10:23

Divine Exchange

Dear God

_____

_____

_____

_____

_____

Dear Daughter

_____

_____

_____

_____

_____

WIDOW MAKER

Dear God,

Two months ago, my husband scared me to death. Because of chest pains, an ambulance rushed him to the hospital. To save his life, Dr. Kwan performed two heart catheterizations, and implanted three stents in his left anterior descending artery—the widow-maker.

A battery of medications and change in diet stabilized Ron's physical condition. But emotionally, depression and anger now control his moods.

When I express my concerns, he says, "I'm fine."

End of discussion.

Ron's mental health impacts every aspect of our lives. He used to love his work, but now he dreads each day. He mopes and complains. Hour after hour he wastes in a stupor watching TV. Golf no longer satisfies, because he's too tired to play. He avoids friends. And sex. God, he's not *fine*. He is out of circulation.

While he's in denial, I feel helpless and lonely, like a living widow. God, will you please help me?

Donna

My Dear Donna,

How difficult and scary for you to face this sudden crisis. Fear of losing your husband and best friend presented you with one of life's most difficult challenges—facing questions of eternity. To complicate matters, his emotional aftershock left you feeling helpless. Coping with denial can be as difficult as enduring the physical trauma.

You are not alone. All through history, man has struggled with denial.[1] Ron's fear of dying causes him to live a lie.[2] Yet, he only fools himself and creates a barrier between you.[3] He can't see how he hurts you.

Spiritual forces rooted in pride and destruction sway your lives, causing Ron to refuse advice,[4] but when he realizes that his life rests in My loving hands, he'll see the man in the mirror. When he is ready to bring his sorrow and fear to Me, I will be there to listen to his heart.[5] When he accepts My sovereignty over his life and death, I will set him free from fear and give him the gift of a meaningful and joyful life.

Precious Donna, speak truth in love to Ron about this issue.[6] You must extend abundant grace as he comes to terms with his own mortality. Stay on your knees. Pray to break the cycle of denial that grips his hard-hearted spirit. Otherwise, this barrier between you will fester.[7]

---

[1] The Life Recovery Bible, (IL: Tyndale House Publishing, Inc., 1998), 57
[2] Ibid., 795; 1371
[3] Ibid, 1415, 1373
[4] Ibid.,1130
[5] Ibid., 1134
[6] Ephesians 4:15
[7] Ibid., 1373

Wait for Ron to be willing for Me to work in his life.

Wait for My perfect timing to answer your prayers.

Wait on Me.[8] I promise to comfort you each lonely moment.

Love,
God

God's Promise: Isaiah 40:31

> Those who trust in the Lord will find new strength. They will soar high on wings like eagles. They will run and not grow weary. They will walk and not faint.

---

[8] Psalm 27:14

Divine Exchange

Dear God

_____

_____

_____

_____

_____

Dear Daughter

_____

_____

_____

_____

_____

PINK SLIP

Dear God,

I hate my job. My boss thinks she owns me. Since she has no family, her career became her entire life. In her opinion, she's entitled to all of my time. She expects me to avail myself to meet her agenda whenever she calls, day or night. If I plan personal activities instead of working overtime, she considers me disloyal and believes that *I am not committed to the company.*

She scares me and intimidates me with pink slips.

Jack thinks I should keep the job regardless of the negative impact on our marriage and children. According to him, we *need the money.* I don't agree, but if I quit, I feel disloyal.

I just can't do this anymore. For $58,000 plus bonus, insurance benefits, 401K, cell phone, computer, and company car, I sold my soul to the devil. God, if this frenzied lifestyle continues, I'll have a nervous breakdown. What should I do?

Dianna

My Dear Dianna,

Your constant furrowed brow reveals that your work life has spun out of control. Naturally, married to a nonbeliever, your priorities differ from Jack's, and you walk a fine line with each decision. You must choose between obeying My Word or obeying man. Since I am your final authority,[1] you must follow My ways,

---

[1] Daniel 7:13-14

even when Jack disagrees with My precepts based on a biblical principle called *obedient disobedience.*[2]

Dianna, money poses a valid consideration—but not your only consideration. This challenge you face offers you a perfect time to examine my Word. Keep asking for My guidance and wisdom as you and Jack make a decision for your future. Keep on seeking, and you will find answers. Keep on knocking, and the next right door will be opened.[3]

As you seek to align your career decision with My will, consider these principles:

- People must always be considered above the making of money.

- People must always be more important than products.

- Keep away from pride in your own programs, plans, and successes.

- Remember that My will and Word must never be compromised.

- Do what is right, no matter what the cost.

- Be involved in businesses that provide worthwhile products or services—not just things that feed the world's desires.[4]

Dianna, I care about every detail of this decision and your future. Would I not command My angels to care for you if you asked?[5] When you acknowledge Me in all your ways, I will keep your path straight.[6] Live generously by faith, without fear, trusting in My sovereign, tender loving care for you.

---

[2] Bill Crowder, *Daniel: Spiritual Living in A Secular Culture* (Thomas Nelson, Inc,1982), 26

[3] Matthew 7:7-8

[4] *Life Application Bible, NIV, Large Print* (Tyndale House Publishers, Inc. and Zondervan Publishing House, 1995), 2763

[5] Luke 4:10

[6] Proverbs 3:6

Precious daughter, I love you—always and forever.

Love,
God

God's Promise: Jeremiah 1:19

They will fight you, but they will fail. For I am with you, and I will take care of you.

Divine Exchange

Dear God

_____

_____

_____

_____

_____

_____

Dear Daughter

_____

_____

_____

_____

_____

_____

YESTERDAY
ALL MY TROUBLES SEEMED SO FAR AWAY

Dear God,

I used to think you were good, but now I have serious doubts. In one beat of my heart, my entire life flattened like an EKG.

Wasn't it just yesterday my precious grandchildren warmed my heart as we chased Poochie near the lake? The fragrance of roses in full bloom delighted my senses as I sipped wine on the veranda. All the hassles from the divorce were behind me, and I enjoyed the good life on Hysteria Lane—everything to make me happy.

But that was yesterday.

Today, a hospital bed engulfs my body. *Why me, Lord? What did I do to deserve this?* The ER doctor told Justin, "The CAT scan of your mother's brain revealed a hemorrhaged pool of blood inside her brain. Her damaged brain looks bad. You may lose her. Dr. Ryan, the best neurosurgeon in the region, will evaluate her, and he may decide to operate, but because of the location of the blood and the damage done, it is unlikely to be successful."

Boom. Just like that my life changed forever. As the ceiling closes in on me, questions invade my thoughts.

God, why didn't you just let me die on the floor where I collapsed?

Will I be like a vegetable? What if I never walk again? Or talk? Or drive?

What if I never again hug my grandbabies or feel Poochie lick my cheek?

I'm exhausted, God. Fretting and lack of sleep drain my energy. Numbness plagues my right side from head to toe. Every other body part aches. When I'm alone, fear grips my heart. I feel confused, then angry, because I have no husband to help me. When the kids visit, I snap. Justin tries to help by taking charge. Is there no end to his questions that I can't answer? He says I've been here six weeks already, but I don't remember. Alexis pretends everything is normal, but how can I bear another glance at the terror in her eyes?

In the hospital, my roommate heaves to vomit, and I wish I'd gone deaf rather than numb. Instead of the sweet aroma of roses, stench fills the air. I am embarrassed when my sagging, right lower lip drools without warning. Cold, metal machines mirror my constant fears and tears. My stained gown gapes, because I can't tend to my personal needs. I feel humiliated. Worst of all, I had hoped someday to find another husband, but what man could love a woman like me?

God, what did I do to deserve this pain? I feel desperate. What will become of me?[1]

Nancy

My Dear Nancy,

I see your despair, and I am filled with compassion for you.[2] Nothing you did caused this calamity. My precious daughter, I know you would never have chosen this heartache, but I will take care of you. Cling to me when you feel weak. My love and grace will sustain you as we walk through these dark days and scary nights together.

---

[1] Nancy R. Johnson, Healing Ministry Speaker, All Saints Church of Winter Park, Florida, July 29, 2003. www.allsaintswp.com/healingministry
[2] Psalm 103:8a

Although you may not yet understand, I will raise you up for My good purposes.[3] So, continue to trust Me now, as you always have. Even with all you suffer, I am with you always.[4] Not only will you survive this ordeal, you will flourish like a tree planted along a riverbank bearing fruit each season.[5] Doctor Ryan will be amazed at My greatness.[6]

Growing in love, Nancy, you will develop a keen discernment of My presence. As your emotions heal, you will learn the true meaning of forgiveness. Painful wounds from your divorce will fade to benign scars. Instead of material possessions, people in your life will become your treasures, and you will be rich with dear friendships unlike any you have ever known.

When you can't read, I will liven your life with music and soothe your frayed nerves by sending friends to share Scripture. Phone calls, notes, flowers, and warm wishes all reveal My loving touch. I will hug you through your children and grandchildren, for I have ordained all the days of your life.[7]

Through this journey, your heart will give way to spiritual quickening. As you come to believe without a doubt that I am sovereign[8] over your life, you will discover true freedom. With each step of faith, your spiritual roots will grow deeper and stronger.

Come to Me now, my child. Curl up in My lap. Cry away your fears. Then, when you are ready, be still and know that I am God.[9]

---

[3] Romans 9:17
[4] Matthew 28:20b
[5] Psalm 1:3
[6] Luke 9:43
[7] Psalm 139:16
[8] Jeremiah 32:17
[9] Psalm 46:10

I am here with you to nourish your soul. Experience the depth of My peace. Allow My Spirit to permeate yours—Daddy's here.[10]

Love,
God

God's Promise: Psalm 37:23-24

The Lord directs the steps of the godly. He delights in every detail of their lives. Though they stumble, they will never fall, for the Lord holds them by the hand.

---

[10] Romans 8:15b

Divine Exchange

Dear God

_____

_____

_____

_____

_____

_____

Dear Daughter

_____

_____

_____

_____

_____

_____

Jeanne LeMay

STRANGERS IN THE NIGHT

Dear God I'm Desperate

ALONE TOGETHER

Dear God,

Alone together—that's how I describe my relationship with Josh. We've been married eight years, and our son, Chris, turned five yesterday. Between Chris and our adorable baby, Kayla, kids consume our lives.

At mealtime, I feel like a short-order cook trying to please everyone. At bedtime, Chris refuses to sleep in his own bed, and he crawls into our bed, between Josh and me. When Kayla wakes up crying, I bring her into bed with everybody else. Josh, frustrated with little feet jabbing his ribs all night, gets angry with me, and retreats to the sofa.

Josh and I never enjoy quality adult time together. Our marriage has gone downhill from the moment I said *I do*, and I'm beginning to not care. Why on earth are we are staying together? We don't fight. We don't discuss anything. We coexist, alone together.

God, I know you hate divorce.[1] What should I do?

Angela

Dear Angela,

I am relieved that you came to me early in your strained relationship with Josh. I know you feel disappointed. You probably don't realize that Josh's feelings hurt, too. Like many men, he has difficulty expressing his pain. You have both lost the communion

---

[1] Malachi 2:16

of love you once found so dear to your hearts that drew you to marriage.

Since you and Josh both came from broken homes, you missed the opportunity to learn loving and effective skills to resolve family issues. To complicate matters, many of your friends consider divorce as the best solution to problems, but that choice will not result in happiness for you or Josh. In fact, the decision to end a marriage complicates every aspect of your lives. Not only are you left with your initial unresolved problems, divorce piles trouble upon troubles.[2] Thoughts of ending your marriage covenant must be held captive, for a house divided will fall.[3]

My precious daughter, you are at a turning point, and I know your heart.[4] You would do anything to save your marriage, so I offer you now My tested and proven wisdom[5] for a successful marriage and healthy family.

When you are ready, we'll begin by searching your heart.[6]

What grievances stand between you Josh? Did he fail to bring flowers or bestow a needed compliment? Did you sustain a grudge when he left you feeling alone to sleep on the couch? What words did he carelessly fling that punctured your heart?

I know your list is long, but that's okay. Exhaust your gripes as you journal to Me. As you list his transgressions against you, observe the baggage that blocks intimacy. Give thought to your own ways and unrealistic expectations, for each heart knows its own bitterness.[7]

Precious, are you ready to choose to forgive Josh?[8] Forgiveness seems hard and unfair after all he's done, but I encourage you to strain to move in that direction, and I will help

---

[2] Psalm 25:17
[3] Luke 11:17
[4] Acts 15:8-9
[5] Proverbs 3:13-14
[6] Psalm 139:23-24
[7] Proverbs 14:8-10
[8] Matthew 18:21-22

you wrestle through every transgression. I will patiently bring you through the pain and savor your tears.

Angela, My dear, have you asked Josh if he holds any resentment toward you? Have you hurt his feelings? Do you remember when you called him a jerk and complained that he doesn't make enough money? Do you recall when you asked him if you looked fat, and he hesitated to answer? You thought he was disgusted with your body, but he was admiring the woman he loves.

Do you realize that you nag him beyond reason about watching sports on television? He deserves a reasonable time to relax from a stressful day at the office. Do you remember when you were impatient with him for wanting to sleep in his own bed— without children? He's frustrated, because he can't express his overflowing love for you with Chris and Kayla between you. That issued has remained unresolved and festering for nearly two years.

Will you take time to reflect on these things? Then, when you are ready, ask Josh to forgive you. Barriers that block affection begin to dissolve when you forgive each other as I have forgiven you.[9]

Regarding adorable Chris and Kayla, I know you delight in them as I delight in you,[10] but they need discipline.[11] They control your family, like a tail wagging the dog. I intended for Josh to be the head of your household,[12] and I created you to partner with him.[13]

As you turn your hearts toward Me, the stress between you will decrease, you will restore intimacy, your marriage will flourish, and your family will be blessed.

Most important, my precious child, as you draw closer to Me, you and Josh will no longer be alone together for I have a unique

---

[9] Ephesians 4:32
[10] Psalm 149:4
[11] Proverbs 23:13-14
[12] Ephesians 5:23
[13] Genesis 2:18

mission for your marriage[14] that will unify your hearts with mine and give your lives meaning. As you discover your common purpose together, you both will begin to enjoy spiritual intimacy beyond measure.

Love,
God

God's Promise: Jeremiah 33:3

> Ask Me, and I will tell you remarkable secrets you do not know about things to come.

---

[14] Clint & Penny A. Bragg, Your Marriage, God's Mission—Discovering Your Spiritual Purpose Together, Kregel Publications (Oct, 2017) www.MarriageonaMission.com

Divine Exchange

Dear God

Dear Daughter

AMAZING GRACE

Dear God,

Three years ago, my husband of 17 years divorced me to marry a younger woman—his secret mistress.

I still feel angry and bitter. Our 15 year-old daughter, Amanda, in her youthful wisdom, said, "Mom, get over it. When are you going to forgive Dad and get a life?"

I know in my heart Amanda is right. Yet, I have no idea how to forgive him—he betrayed me and hurt me deeper than a buried secret.

God, I hate what Brian did to me. How on earth do I forgive him?

Amanda

My Dear Amanda

I know the depth of heartache your husband caused when he left you, and I feel your pain. I also see beyond your past and know that you are a wonderful woman with potential for a full and productive life. Even without him.

The sad truth is that Brian chose to do what he did according to his own distorted belief system. In his mind, he believed he made the best decision for his life, leaving you with a difficult choice—forgive or hold a grudge. Either way, one ironic truth remains. When you don't forgive, *you* are the one robbed of joy. Facing that truth will begin to set you free.[1]

Amanda, I hear your thoughts. *Why should I forgive him? He doesn't deserve an ounce of consideration after what he did to me.*

Forgiving Brian does not mean that what he did wasn't wrong. You simply choose to forgive him, because I forgave you. I trod your sins underfoot and hurled your iniquities into the depths of the sea.[2] Now, I delight in showing you mercy and compassion.

As I have treated you, Amanda, you must treat others.

Forgive, and you will be forgiven. Be merciful, just as I show mercy, so it will be given to you. For with the measure you use, it will be measured to you.[3] If you forgive others when they sin against you, so will I also forgive you, but if you do not forgive others their sins, I will not forgive yours.[4] If you judge or condemn others, you too will be judged.[5]

Forgiveness will wind you off the slippery slope you're on toward a secure path, and I promise to be with you through the process. Are you *willing* now to examine your own heart and learn how to forgive?

To start, admit that Brian indeed sinned against you. He left the partner of his youth and ignored the covenant he made with you before Me.[6] He threw caution to the wind, disregarding the impact of his choice on others as well as consequences he would face in the future.

Amanda, for you to maintain intimacy with Me, it's important for you to search your own heart.[7] Have you allowed a bitter root of judgment to fester against Brian? Are you ready to surrender the whole situation to Me so I may shine My guiding light on all secrets hidden in darkness? I'll expose the motives of each man's

---

[1] John 8:32
[2] Micah 7:18-19
[3] Matthew 7:2
[4] Matthew 6:14-15
[5] Luke 6:37
[6] Proverbs 2:17
[7] Psalm 139:23-24

heart[8] and in My perfect timing and way, I judge all sexual immorality.[9] Will you trust Me to be God in your life?

My precious daughter, by My grace love Brian with this act of forgiveness.[10] In that way, you reveal My selfless love to others. Receive My empowering presence to enable you to set your beautiful heart free to love again.

Love,
God

God's Promise: Psalm 84:11b

The Lord will withhold no good thing from those who do what is right.

---

[8] 1 Corinthians 4:5
[9] Hebrews 13:4b
[10] 2 Thessalonians 1:12

Divine Exchange

Dear God

Dear Daughter

DUST BUNNIES IN MY HEART

Dear God,

As I glance at my *prince charming* of 29 years and 73 days, my marriage feels barren and cold like endless winter. His lifetime of manual labor wore out his hands as well as his morale. What's left of his hair turned a drab shade of grey. A soft, flabby belly now replaces the firm abs of his youth. For both of us, our marriage has been a disappointment.[1]

When did our honeymoon end? When did our joy freeze? I don't remember. One day everything just changed. A string of strained days turned to months, and months turned into years. We'll never reach happily-ever-after.

I'm desperate to be loved again.

Kim

My Dear Kim,

I remember your wedding day as if it were yesterday. The candlelit church held a sweet fragrance redolent with love. Everyone stood breathless in anticipation as the organ played, *Here Comes the Bride*. Love looked stunning on you.

Then the mundane moments of life robbed you like a thief. Disappointments grew over the years, and transgressions collected

---

[1] Dena Dyer and Laurie Barker Copeland, The Groovy Chicks Road Trip to Love, (CO: Cook Communications Ministries, 2006), 135

like dust bunnies under the bed. Random acts of kindness were hung out to dry. The monotonous humdrum of life obliterated your thoughtful words and deeds toward one another.

I remember Vince's gaze and delight as you swished down the aisle on your father's strong right arm. Light and hope danced in your eyes. You created memories to treasure for a lifetime.

"I, Kimberly Taylor Reninger

Take you, Vincent Thomas DeMarco

To be my wedded husband

To have and to hold from this day forward.

For better, for worse, for richer, for poorer

In sickness and in health

To love and to cherish

Until death do us part.

And hereto I pledge you my faithfulness.

This is my solemn vow."[2]

My precious Kim, look at your wedding band. Do you remember snuggling with Vince in the jewelry store making your ring selections? When he slid the slender gold band onto your trembling finger to seal your wedding vows, a shiver trickled down your spine. I saw your tears of joy as you whispered *"I do."*

In My eyes, your wedding rings exchanged that day indicate the outward and visible sign of an inward bond uniting your two hearts in endless love. Those circlets of pure gold symbolize your faithful and changeless affection forevermore. Do you realize that your *holy matrimony* represents your testimony to Me? The temptation to break your promise of the lifelong commitment you made to Vince now tests your faith. This binding oath would not be necessary if marriage were an easy path.

---

[2] www.foreverwed.com

My beautiful bride, the wedding march grew silent, and you now step to a different cadence. Your gown has changed to jeans. But, I am still with you for better and for worse. That is my solemn vow to you. Take hold of My strong right arm now as I walk with you toward Vince and rekindle the twinkle in your eyes.

Love,
God

God's Promise: Ecclesiastes 4:12

A person standing alone can be attacked and defeated, but two can stand back-to-back and conquer. Three are even better, for a triple-braided cord is not easily broken.

Divine Exchange

Dear God

Dear Daughter

FOOL AROUND

Dear God,

I'm afraid to admit, but I think I married a fool. My Billy's ways seem right to him, but he will not listen to advice.[1] He loves to air his own opinions.[2] He is clueless about his negative impact on our relationship. In fact, he doesn't care.

He assumes there is only one way to relate—his way. If I'm unhappy about our relationship, he thinks there is something wrong with me. He ignores my suggestions that his thinking might be flawed or that his behavior might be inappropriate.[3]

Billy will never confess or repent of wrongdoing. Why would he? He believes he is *always* right. This mind-set is at the very core of his being, and it controls all he is and everything he does.[4]

God, I was wrong to ignore your advice about marriage. I was wrong to not wait for You to bring a suitable husband for me. Instead of rushing into marriage, I should have developed my character to know the gifts and talents you purposed for me. But no, I couldn't wait. I had to have Billy. He was charming. Fun. Flattering. Lovable. Mr. High School Hunk. God's gift to women. Mr. Popularity. That's my Billy. Immature, irresponsible Billy. The bona fide fool about whom you warned me in Proverbs. Sometimes I feel like his mother instead of his wife.

---

[1] Proverbs 12:15
[2] Proverbs 18:2
[3] Jan Silvious, *Fool-Proofing Your Life: Wisdom for Untangling Your Most Difficult Relationships* (CO: Waterbrook Press, 1998), 29-30
[4] Ibid. 30

God, I am so sorry I turned against You. Now my life is chaotic and difficult. If you will help me, I promise to do what you say now. I have learned my lesson the foolish way.

Traci

My Dear Traci,

Since you are eager to follow My advice, and Billy is blazing his own trail, you are as different as a PC and a MAC, operating from different platforms. But, you have tuned your ear to My voice, so I will help you untangle your relationship until you become compatible.

Traci, there is much for you to learn from your circumstances. In your interactions with Billy, you must be shrewd as a serpent and innocent as a dove. [5] Your goal cannot be to change him. No matter what choices he makes, you must find your freedom in Me that allows you to be the woman I intend for you to be.[6] Instead of letting Billy determine your identity, I will redefine you as My daughter and fill you with My love.

Your personal goal must be to read My Word and allow My truth to renew your mind.[7] Proverbs will give you warnings to help you avoid snares in your marriage and provide you with principles for making sound decisions. With pure motives, your choices will please Me.

As you walk humbly in My ways and keep My commandments, I will place in you a Godly heart toward your husband. When his behavior seems foolish, instead of becoming dismayed, you will possess My keen discernment to make excellent judgments and timely decisions. As you distinguish My

[5] Matthew 10:16
[6] Jan Silvious, 76
[7] Romans 12:2

Truth that leads to freedom, you will again be able to enjoy Billy's charming and lovable qualities that first attracted you to him.

As far as it depends on you, My precious daughter, live in peace with Billy while I reveal Myself to him through your right behavior.[8] With My edifying words on your lips, he will be blessed by your gentle encouragement.[9]

Most importantly, Traci, as a believing wife you bring My Holiness to your marriage—Billy may be saved because of you.[10]

Love,
God

God's Promise: Joshua 1:9

Be strong and courageous! Do not be afraid or discouraged, for the Lord your God is with you wherever you go.

---

[8] Romans 12:18
[9] Ephesians 4:29
[10] 1 Corinthians 7:14, 16

Divine Exchange

Dear God

Dear Daughter

NOT TONIGHT HONEY

Dear God,

I dread sex. As a matter of fact, I'd rather have migraines. When Chad approaches with hopes of physical intimacy, my head pounds with negative thoughts. Guilt and obligation jockey for my attention. Do I meet Chad's needs, or turn my back on him with another headache?

I feel tense, upset and disengaged—like a prostitute who refuses to kiss on the lips.

Frustrated, we live alone together as strangers.

"I'm not important to you, or you wouldn't always have those migraines," he snarls.

Likewise, I feel unimportant to him. For me, physical intimacy is impossible without emotional connection. He refuses to join me in counseling, so I'm losing hope for our marriage.

God, will you help me?

Stephanie

My Dear Stephanie,

You are not alone—many women struggle with sexual intimacy in their marriages. Strife between you and Chad caused isolation and sadness. With your spirit crushed, you lost hope.

My heart breaks, because My design for marriage includes freedom for you to enjoy physical, emotional, and spiritual intimacy.[1] Husbands and wives who uplift, bless, and affirm one another[2] develop a nurturing environment in which to flourish. I see every aspect of your lives together,[3] and your sexual problems represent warning signs[4] of deeper concerns that need to be addressed.

Stephanie, because you have humbled yourself and turned to Me, I will help you through this difficult season of your life.[5] I AM the cornerstone[6]—your solid foundation essential for you to thrive. Unless you build your home on the solid rock of My word, you labor in vain.[7]

During this crisis, are you are willing to stand firm[8] on your vows to protect the marriage I provided for you? Are you ready to persevere and look for opportunities to encourage and edify Chad rather than turn away in defeat? May I help you shift your attitude toward him from blame to compassion?

My dear daughter, I'll help you forgive and begin anew. Share your tender emotions and vulnerable heart with Me now. Pour forth every bottled up sorrow for I know how you feel.[9] I'll listen and touch your deepest heartache with gentle compassion.[10]

---

[1] Life Recovery Bible, Song of Songs Recovery Theme: The Joy of Commited Love, 838.

[2] Ephesians 5:1-2a; 31-33

[3] Hebrews 4:13

[4] 2 Peter 3:17-18

[5] Ecclesiastes 3:1

[6] Matthew 21:42

[7] Psalm 127:1

[8] Ephesians 6:11

[9] Isaiah 53:3

[10] Matthew 9:36

As you seek to know Me and love Me with all your heart,[11] I'll direct your steps, because I care about every detail of your life.[12] I promise to protect you, redeem your life from destruction, and crown you with loving kindness and tender mercies.[13]

Love,
God

God's Promise: Romans 15:5

> God, who gives patience and encouragement, helps you live in complete harmony with each other, as is fitting for followers of Jesus Christ.

---

[11] Matthew 22:37
[12] Psalm 37:23
[13] Psalm 103:4

Divine Exchange

Dear God

Dear Daughter

SEVENTEEN ROSES

Dear God,

This morning when Tyler came into the kitchen, I expected a hug and a card for our anniversary. Or maybe Godiva chocolates and a bouquet of seventeen roses. Instead, he dropped an emotional bomb.

"Jenna, I'm leaving. I want a divorce," He turned his back and walked toward the front door.

"Tyler, stop." I followed him pulling his arm, but he wouldn't face me or look into my eyes. Too shocked for tears, I stared from the porch as he drove down the street and out of my life. The sting of his words triggered heart palpitations and ripped apart my soul.

Feeling helpless and dizzy, I stumbled aimlessly from room to room. *What just happened here? What did I do wrong? I don't want a divorce. I love Tyler.* Sobs overcame me until mountains of wadded tissues surrounded me on all sides.

Spent from crying, suspicions haunted me. *Who is she? When did he pack? How long has his scheme been planned?* Then a wave of anger swept through me like a storm. *How dare he dump me like trash? I hate Tyler.*

God, I need help. I'm confused and afraid. I feel so alone.

Jenna

My Dear Jenna,

My heart grieves as you suffer. How shocked you must feel. Tyler's betrayal jarred your emotions and pierced your heart like an arrow. No wonder questions and anger torment your mind. As your thoughts ramble, you see no hope.

Jenna, I know you feel vulnerable, but don't lose heart[1] for I am with you. Share your troubles with Me one by one, because I care about every detail of your life and watch over you as you lie awake and as you sleep.[2] Call upon Me, and I will answer you.[3]

I promise to comfort you when you cry.[4]

I promise to protect you when you feel afraid.[5]

I promise to stay close by your side whenever you feel alone. [6]

My love feels softer than a mother's kiss upon her baby's forehead and sounds more splendid than a symphony. If I could paint My love for you, the pallet of colors would resemble exquisite jewels. My love tastes far more decadent than the finest chocolates. It's fragrance—sweeter than seventeen roses.

Do you know how deeply I love you? My affection for you defies comprehension.[7] You are always on My mind. Take My hand, Jenna, and I will help you. You are never alone.[8]

Love,
God

God's Promise: Psalm 46:1

God is our refuge and strength, always ready to help in times of trouble.

---

[1] Hebrews 12:2
[2] Psalm 4:8
[3] Jeremiah 33:3
[4] Isaiah 49:13
[5] Psalm 40:11
[6] Psalm 23:4
[7] Ephesians 3:19
[8] Matthew 28:20b

Divine Exchange

Dear God

_____

_____

_____

_____

_____

_____

Dear Daughter

_____

_____

_____

_____

_____

_____

RUNAWAY BRIDE

Dear God,

Where do disheartened brides go to run away?

Friday, when my husband and I got into a heated argument with both of us yelling and screaming, out of fear I tried to leave. Angry and forceful, he trapped me in the corner of the kitchen and held my arms behind my back.

"Where do you think you are going," Jeff bullied.

Frantic about what he would do next, I threatened to call the police again. Disgusted, he flung my hands down and left the room.

Unwanted thoughts of Jeff's endless, hateful word-darts battered my mind.

If you hadn't done that, I wouldn't be mad. It's all your fault.

If you hadn't said that first, I wouldn't have to yell at you.

If you didn't yap on the phone all day, I wouldn't have to hang up the receiver on your stupid friends.

A shiver unsettled my heart as I recalled bitter memories of our first anniversary. With the excitement of a new bride, I planned a special dinner in our home—just the two of us—to rekindle our romance. With the preparations for his favorite foods well underway, and music drifting through the air, I slipped into my wedding gown for the occasion, delighted it still zipped. When my handsome groom arrived for the celebration with love twinkling in his eyes, I felt hopeful, and my heart melted.

Within five minutes, an uncomfortable silence between us replaced the music. *What did I do wrong this time?* Before I had a chance to serve the top layer of cake that had been carefully preserved since our wedding, he grabbed his plate, stomped off to our bedroom and slammed the door, leaving me feeling alone and dejected. Tears stained my gown.

As my thoughts returned from the disappointing memory, my body convulsed at the reality of my current situation. I'm ashamed and embarrassed to tell anyone about our marriage, but who would believe me even if I did tell the truth? After all, Jeff's a successful businessman, we live in a stunning home in our gated community, and we're members of the West Hysteria Country Club.

For the next two days, I wandered through the house dazed and frightened, wondering what he would do next. He didn't speak to me, inflicting another dose of punishing silent treatment. Finally, on Sunday morning, after days of emotional freeze-out, he dressed for church as if nothing had happened. Seeing me still in my nightgown, his voice brimming with kindness, he asked, "Aren't we going to church this morning?"

Upon arrival at the church, as I headed to the small chapel for prayer, I told Jeff I'd meet him in the sanctuary. When Maggie greeted me with a smile and hug, years of bottled-up tension exploded into tears.

Maggie said, "What on earth happened? What's wrong? Do you want me to get Jeff?"

My sobs provided no answer as tears drenched my face and Maggie's pretty dress.

"Do you want me to take you home?"

"No. NO. I can't go there. I can't go there. I'm never going home again."

As my body tremored from confusion and fear, Susan chimed in, "Do you want to stay at my house for a few days? You can decide what to do after you rest."

"Okay," I muttered.

As Susan drove me home to pack a bag, I wondered if Jeff still sat alone in the church. She suggested I call him. So with shaky hands, I reached for my cell phone, dialed and left a voicemail.

"I'm fine. Staying with a friend for a few days. Don't try to call me. I'll call you."

After being nursed by Susan's gentle care during the weekend, I knew I could *never* return home, so she arranged for me to borrow a friend's condo at the beach for the next four days. When we arrived, I clung to her like a frightened four-year old child. Vomit seeped into my throat.

In the next few seconds, I weighed my options.

Do I stay here completely alone and terrified, or do I go back home to domestic violence?

Deep inside I knew my only choice. As horrid as running away seemed, returning home would be worse. Sadly, I gathered my few clothes and belongings scattered helter-skelter in Susan's car. With a lump in my throat, I waved goodbye as she drifted out of sight. Opening the door of the dark and musty condo, shame shrouded me like a dirty blanket. In the dead silence, as I collapsed onto the sofa, Mother's terse words haunted me. *It's your own d*** fault, Jeanne.*

God, why do I feel battered? Jeff never hit me. I love him, and I hate him. If only I hadn't provoked him, then I would be safe and sound at home instead of floundering in this strange place. He told me he loves me, so what am I doing here alone and hopeless?

Now that Jeff changed the locks, I'm homeless, hanging by a thread, popping sleeping pills day and night to cope. God, where, oh where, do I find comfort for my ramshackle heart?

Whatever happens to me now, I don't care—I give up.

Jeanne

My Dear Jeanne,

I hear every cry of your heart and see your crushed spirit.[1] You longed for a happy marriage and a promising life, but your hopes have been dashed by a series of endless disappointments and chaotic circumstances.

Many people you trusted throughout your life proved to be unpredictable and unreliable. Driven by selfish motives, their unwise decisions and string of lies harmed your tender heart. Sadly, betrayal after betrayal destroyed your confidence to trust even Me. After all you've endured, I understand why you doubt that I'd come through for you and keep My promises.

Although fear threatens to hinder you, the secret to trusting Me rests in getting to know Me personally. My precious daughter, you have already taken the first step. By writing to me, you admitted that you are powerless over your problems and your life has become unmanageable. Your humble act of surrender indicated that you believe My supernatural strength can help, and you want to trust Me. You are ready to walk hand-in-hand with Me no matter what life brings forth.[2]

As we begin our journey together, place your trembling hand in My secure hold. Little by little, I'll comfort you and calm your fears.[3] With My steadfast love, your brokenness will begin to heal. As I carefully watch over your coming and going[4] and treat you with tender kindness,[5] you will start to believe that you are worthy of love. The more you experience My goodness and grace, the more My seeds of love will produce trust in your heart.

Pour out your concerns to Me in prayer. I will always hear your cries as you share your needs. Practice daily journaling,

---

[1] Psalm 34:17-18
[2] Life Recovery Bible, Steps 1-3, A9
[3] Zephaniah 3:17
[4] Psalm 121:7-8
[5] Psalm 37:39-40

placing your pain and burdens in My sovereign care. Then, read your Bible starting with Psalms and absorb My words of tender love for you. By renewing your mind,[6] peace begins to replace your fearful thoughts and worries.

Seek first My Kingdom, and I will give you *everything* you need to navigate this crisis and for your future.[7] Reflect on the meaning of scriptures. My Holy Spirit, your wise counselor, will protect you and lead you in all truth.[8] As I meet your needs day by day, and you learn that I am honest, trustworthy, and faithful, your confidence to trust Me with your fragile heart will grow stronger.

Continue to pursue righteousness, faithfulness, love and peace by seeking Me in prayer, reading My Word, and journaling daily. Evaluate your thoughts, words, and deeds against My Word as your plumb line, and do what is right in My eyes. Trust and obey, for there's no other way. With Me as your source of security, My victory over seemingly impossible circumstances becomes available to you.

Walk humbly with Me,[9] and I will make a way for you even though there seems to be no way.[10] For I am about to redeem your past and do something new—a Divine Exchange.

In place of your shattered dreams, I will give you hope for a future with meaning and purpose.

Instead of mourning and despair, I will bring forth joyous blessings and festive praise. A crown of beauty will replace the ashes.[11]

My precious daughter, rest in My love for you. Be still and know I that am God,[12] for all I have planned and purposed for you stands true forever.[13] I promise to help and encourage you, for I am

---

[6] Romans 12:2
[7] Matthew 6:33
[8] John 14:17a
[9] Micah 6:8
[10] Isaiah 43:19
[11] Isaiah 61:3
[12] Psalm 46:10
[13] Isaiah 14:24

with you, and I will not fail you or abandon you.[14]Acknowledge Me in all your ways as I make your path straight[15] and lavish you with blessing upon blessing. [16]

Love,
God

God's Promise: Matthew 11:28-29

> Come to Me all of you who are weary and carry heavy burdens, and I will give you rest. Take My yoke upon you. Let Me teach you, because I am humble and gentle at heart, and you will find rest for your soul.

---

[14] Joshua 1:5
[15] Proverbs 3:6
[16] Psalm 31:19

Divine Exchange

Dear God

_____

_____

_____

_____

_____

Dear Daughter

_____

_____

_____

_____

_____

FROM THE AUTHOR

Dear Readers,

Do your circumstances cause you to feel discouraged, helpless or shamed?

Take heart, you are not alone. I, too, have been desperate.

When I reached out for God, He touched me with tender compassion and comforted my broken heart. He knew each tear before I cried. He held me close as I learned to trust His promises to meet all of my needs.

Through the book *Dear God I'm Desperate – Women Have Issues God Has Answers*, I hope you learn, as I did, to navigate through the difficult circumstances plaguing your life with God's help. May you, too, experience His Divine Exchange of faith for fear, dignity for shame and hope for despair.

Won't you join me in seeking first the Kingdom of God?

Jeanne

246

www.ingramcontent.com/pod-product-compliance
Lightning Source LLC
Chambersburg PA
CBHW060917040426
42445CB00011B/671